A Straightforward Guide to

Bailiff Law

A Guide for Creditors and Debtors

By Anthony Reeves

Published by Straightforward Publishing in 2016

Printed by 4edge www.4edge.co.uk

ISBN: 978-1847165954

Contents

Historical Background

The term "bailiff" was used by the Normans for the officer responsible for executing the decisions of a court. The Saxons had called this officer a "reeve". The duties of the bailiff included serving summonses, orders and warrants. The district within which the bailiff operated was called his "bailiwick"; this term has continued to the present day.

During the Norman period in England, the Saxon and Norman populations became mixed and the use of the term "reeve" came to be limited to "shire-level courts" and this led to the use of the name "sheriff"; the term bailiff tended to be used in relation to lower courts.

Courts were not always concerned with legal matters and often handled administrative matters for the area within their jurisdiction. A bailiff of a manor might oversee the manor's lands and buildings, collecting its rents, managing its accounts, and running its farms.

In the 20th century, the court system was restructured with the "assize courts"[1] taking some of the powers of the shire courts and became the high court; the remaining elements of the shire court took over the

---

[1] The courts of assize were periodic courts held around England and Wales until 1972, when together with the quarter sessions (local county courts held four times per year), they were abolished by the Courts Act 1971 and replaced by a single permanent Crown Court. The assizes exercised both civil and criminal jurisdiction, though most of their work was on the criminal side.

powers of the "hundred courts"[2], to form County Courts. The High Court acquired the sheriffs and the county court the bailiffs. "Sheriffs" in 2003 acquired the title "High Court Enforcement Officers" with the passing of the Courts Act 2003.

With the introduction of the Tribunals, Courts and Enforcement Act 2007 ("TCE Act 2007"), the term "Enforcement Agent" was introduced as the general term to refer to bailiffs (both of the High Court and County Court). A High Court Enforcement Officer is an individual who has been authorised by the Ministry of Justice to enforce High Court judgments; they are not employed by the Ministry of Justice whereas County Court bailiffs are employed civil servants and paid a salary.

****

---

[2]   Under the Saxons, each shire or county in England was divided into a number of hundreds" which were made up of ten tithings each. The tithings were groups of ten families of freeholders. The hundred was governed by a high constable and had its own local court called the "Hundred Court".

Introduction

This book is not designed to be a technical manual on the various intricate legal issues concerning bailiff law but instead it will provide an examination of the basic principles that now govern this area following the changes introduced by the Tribunals, Courts and Enforcement Act 2007 ("TCE") and subsequently by statutory instruments . The provisions that implement the changes are contained in the Taking Control of Goods Regulations 2013 (the "Regulations") and the Civil Procedure Rules ("CPR").

What will be apparent throughout this book is that the term "bailiff" is used when in fact following recent legislation the correct terminology in most situations is "enforcement agent". What will also become apparent is that there are several types of enforcement agent. However, the term "bailiff" has been used for so long and is still the term commonly used, that I will for the most part continue to use the word "bailiff". This was the same when the Woolf reforms of 1999 brought in new terminology in civil court proceedings; it introduced, among other things, the use of the phrase "statements of case" instead of "pleadings" and the name "claimant" instead of "plaintiff". Lawyers after the Woolf reforms continued to use the term "pleadings".

As with many things in law, it is one thing to be told what the law is in a particular area but it is something different to able to recognise what is the right thing to do in a set of circumstances. In the age of the internet there is always easy access to what the law is, but the value of a lawyer is not simply to recite statutes and cases but to be able to assess how the principles will normally be applied in a given set of facts. In some ways, the advent of the internet has changed the focus of what an individual uses a lawyer for; it has not made them redundant but they are (or should be) adapting to a different world. In the area of bailiff law, there are many websites and forums where people (who might not be legally qualified) are giving out advice. The internet forum is the modern day equivalent of the "barrack room" lawyer who you would find holding court in your local pub. That is not to say that all people who post comments and advice have to be qualified lawyers. However what tends to occur with increased communications arising from the growth of the internet is that advice gets circulated and it quickly becomes accepted as "the law", when in reality it is a myth. A good example was that of a bailiff who ignores a "Notice of Removal of Implied Right of Access" and the claim that it would be a trespass. This is not the case. The warrant of control allows a bailiff to attend the debtors premises and to 'take control of goods'. The new Regulations go further and state that any breach or defect of the warrant does not make the enforcement agent, or the person for who he is acting, a trespasser.

The ordinary person, if there is a such a thing, wants to be given a fairly definitive answer as to what to do in a particular situation. In law, the giving of a definitive answer is rare. Most legal opinions these days contain warnings that decisions in courts do not always go as predicted. There is sometimes a marked difference between what in theory the law is and what in practice actually happens. Being able to spot these types of situations is where the experience of a practising lawyer becomes valuable. A debtor may often look at a situation with a view to escaping from what the bailiff is attempting to do and so search for any possible legal loopholes, however tenuous and fanciful the argument might be. A litigant in person (a person not legally represented) is likely to be given more latitude than a lawyer presenting a weak argument. A lawyer is under a professional duty to not mislead the court and to have credible material to support a case being put forward; it should not simply be a case of following instructions without question. A debtor might think that he might as well try an argument to attempt to extricate himself from the clutches of the bailiff because the alternative is the bailiff taking control of his goods. Such an attitude is understandable.

A bailiff is someone authorised (usually by a court) to collect a debt on behalf of a creditor. They are not the same as ordinary debt collectors who do not have any official powers to seize goods.

There are different types of bailiffs:

County Court bailiffs:
These are employed by Her Majesty's Courts and Tribunal Service (HMCTS) and are responsible for enforcing orders by recovering money owed under a county court judgment. They can seize and sell your goods to recover the amount of the debt. They can also effect entry, supervise the possession of the property and

the return of goods under hire purchase agreements, and serve court documents.

Magistrates' Court bailiffs:

They work for the magistrates' court and collect money owed in criminal cases, including fines and money owed in certain non-criminal cases, for example, road traffic penalties. They can seize and sell your goods to recover the amount owed under a fine and community penalty notice. They can also execute warrants of arrest, committal, detention and distress issued by a magistrates' court.

High Court Enforcement officers (HCEO):

They work for the High Court and recover money owed under a High Court judgment or a county court judgment transferred to the High Court. They can seize and sell your goods to cover the amount of the debt. They can also enforce and supervise the possession of property and the return of goods. To become a HCEO, an application has to be made to the Lord Chancellor at the Ministry of Justice. The authorisation is given by a Senior Master of the Queens Bench Division of the High Court on behalf of the Lord Chancellor.

Certificated bailiffs (private bailiffs)

They enforce a variety of debts on behalf of organisations such as local authorities for council tax arrears, Child Support and Child Maintenance Service to collect child maintenance, and HMRC to collect unpaid income tax or VAT. They are often used by magistrates' courts to collect money as above. They can seize and sell your goods to cover the amount of the debt you owe.

They also hold a certificate, granted by a county court judge, which enables them, and them alone, to levy distress for rent, road traffic debts, council tax and non-domestic rates.

****

Part 1

Instructing a bailiff

Before a warrant is issued permitting a bailiff to attend to take control of goods , there will either be a court judgment/court order, court fine, unpaid taxes or a commercial lease permitting the recovery of rent arrears. A common, although not the only, reason for the instruction of a bailiff is to recover the money awarded by court in a civil judgment. Bailiffs are also instructed to recover possession of property. What is sometimes forgotten when debts are being pursued is that a creditor cannot simply instruct a "debt collector" to visit the non-payer and take the debtors goods away. A "debt collector" is not the same as a bailiff. It should be made clear that a debt collector is merely a person who is instructed to chase unpaid debts, usually those which have not been disputed. If a debtor does not or refuses to pay, before taking action to legally collect the debt the creditor will need a court judgment before moving on to instructing a bailiff. The process of obtaining a money judgment will require the issuing of a court claim, usually through the County Court.

The responsibilities of creditors

The National Standards for Taking Control of Goods by Bailiffs published by the Ministry of Justice in April 2014 is not a legally binding document but an important guide to minimum standards. It is important because when complaints are made, for example when complaints are made to the local government ombudsman about the conduct of a bailiff instructed by a local authority, the standards contained in this guide are often used as a useful bench mark as to what should be expected of a bailiff. At the end of this Chapter there is an extract from these National Standards showing the main responsibilities of a creditor.

The key aspect is the statement that the bailiff is acting as the agent of the creditor and ultimately the creditor is responsible for the behaviour of the bailiff. That means that if the bailiff does something wrong then not only could there be action against the bailiff but there could be action against the creditor. It also states that the creditor should consider acting proportionately when instructing a bailiff. To some creditors this will seem rather ironic when they might take the view that the debtor has hardly acted proportionately by not paying what he owes or even anything towards what is due. However, it is a warning against taking a "sledge hammer to crack a nut" or perhaps without having explored a more appropriate method of collecting what is due. The guidelines for considering the appropriateness of referring cases to bailiffs where the debtor is vulnerable avoids people who are not capable of dealing with their own financial affairs from being taken advantage of unfairly. It has got to be sensible to make creditors tell the bailiff what they know about the debtor's circumstances. There is nothing new in this respect as when you instruct a county court bailiff, for example to carry out an eviction, you are always asked ahead of the eviction to warn the bailiff if you feel he might experience difficulties. If you are aware that a debtor is known, for example to be aggressive or has potentially dangerous dogs on the premises, then as the creditor you can understand the bailiff needs to know for his own protection and safety so that appropriate steps can be taken. In the same way, if the debtor is vulnerable, the bailiff should know because if the debtor is known to have mental health issues for example, then he needs be fully prepared when attending to take control of goods. If the bailiff does have the full picture, then he leaves himself open to criticism by the debtor, particularly if the debtor has issues that might lead him to distort what happens when the bailiff visits. In short, the bailiff will expect the creditor to give as much information as possible about the debtor; a failure to pass on material information may well lead to not only the debtor causing the bailiff problems, but ultimately the bailiff company may well consider action against the creditor being negligent in not properly briefing the bailiff when instructing him to take goods.

Instructing Bailiffs - money judgments

A bailiff may be instructed following criminal court proceedings (such as in the Magistrates Court) where a fine is imposed following a conviction and that fine remains unpaid. If a person does not pay Council Tax, the Council applies for a liability order and that is then passed to a bailiff to collect it.

A typical example of a civil matter which could end up with the instruction of a bailiff is a claim through the County Court for an unpaid debt. A creditor wishing to collect a civil debt could:

- obtain a warrant of control in the County Court and instruct a County Court Bailiff ("CCB" - a salaried civil servant employed directly by the court) or
- 'transfer up' the judgment to the High Court for enforcement by an HCEO.

It is important to note that the size of the debt will determine whether a bailiff or High Court Enforcement Officer can enforce the Judgment.

- judgments below £600 may only be enforced by a CCB
- judgments between £600 (including court costs)and £5,000 may be enforced by either a CCB or an HCEO
- judgments above £5,000 may only be enforced by an HCEO

Let us suppose that there is a County Court Judgment ("CCJ") for the sum of £4,000. The creditor can instruct a County Court bailiff or transfer the Judgment up to the High Court for enforcement by a High Court Enforcement Officer ("HCEO").

Instructing a County Court Bailiff

Instructing a county court bailiff is a simple process. It requires the completion of form N323 which is sent to the Court along with the court fee. A copy of form N323 is at the end of this Chapter. If a creditor used Money Claims Online, they can also instruct the bailiff online. The guidance for Claimants who use Money Claims Online explains the process:

Requesting a Warrant online

Please note that whilst the use of MCOL for claim issue against 2 defendants is possible, should you wish to issue a joint warrant of control against both defendants at the same time you will not be able to proceed via MCOL. If you have a joint judgment in a two defendant case and you would like the warrant to be executed against both defendants jointly, you will need to apply for a warrant manually. To do this, please refer to leaflet EX322 for information on how to apply and the fees payable which can be downloaded from www.justice.gov.uk/forms. The application should be sent to the County Court Money Claims Centre (CCMCC) to be processed. Court addresses can be found at https://courttribunalfinder.service.gov.uk/search/

Step 1 - Guidance

Choose the "Warrant" option from Claim Overview page. This brings up a guidance screen, including a warning that the warrant should be for a **maximum of £5000** including costs.

Steps 2, 3 & 4 – Claimant / Defendant Address

Please follow the instructions outlined when entering judgment and select a defendant

Step 5 – Warrant Details

On the "Warrant Details" page the claim judgment figures will show in the top section. The "Balance due at date of this request" box should be completed with the current amount outstanding. You must then type in the amount you would like the bailiff to collect on the warrant.

This amount cannot be more than the outstanding balance due on the judgment and cannot be more than £4930 as the system will not allow the warrant to exceed £5000 (including the warrant fee, which can be confirmed in the EX50 court fees booklet). If you are a Solicitor there will be an opportunity to add your fees as applicable - http://www.justice.gov.uk/courts/procedure-rules/civil/rules/part45-fixed-costs

If the Judgment is for over £5000.00 and payable forthwith or in full by a certain date, you cannot request a warrant unless it relates to the Consumer Credit Act 1974, in which case you may issue a warrant for up to the claim amount.

If The Judgment is for over £5000 and is payable by instalments of less than £5000.00 you can issue a warrant provided the defendant has defaulted on the instalments. The amount of the warrant must be at least one instalment but can be anything up to £5000.00.

At the bottom of the screen there is a box for "Additional Information" where you can provide any extra information that may assist the bailiff in the execution of the warrant. The additional information has a limit of 120 characters and the same conditions apply regarding punctuation as with the POC.

The "additional information box" on the form to request a warrant of control is important because the more information the creditor can provide the bailiff the better the chances of successfully taking control of the debtor's goods, assuming the debtor has goods that can be taken.

15

When a judgment is transferred up for enforcement, it does not become a High Court Judgment but merely the CCJ has been transferred up to the High Court for enforcement by a HCEO. This book does not intend to make too much comment on whether or not a County Court Bailiff is more appropriate than a High Court Enforcement Officer. What can be said though is that it is generally regarded that the County Court bailiff (who is an employee of the court) is less effective or has less time and resources to take control of goods.

Time limit for instructing a bailiff

A creditor should be aware that there is a time limit in which to instruct a bailiff to enforce a Judgment debt. This will not a be a problem in the vast majority of cases because a creditor can take enforcement action up to 6 years from the date of the Judgment. If a creditor wants to take enforcement action on a judgment after 6 years, then permission of the court is required. It may be thought who on earth is going to wait 6 years to enforce a Judgment. It is not uncommon for debt purchasers to be faced with enforcing quite old judgments. The judgment creditor has to be able to persuade the court to exercise it's discretion and grant permission to enforce after 6 years and this will require demonstrating that it is just to do so. The burden of proof is on the creditor to show that it would be just to grant permission.

How to transfer up a County Court Judgment

In the case of a creditor being owed a £4,000 debt and having obtained a CCJ, if it is appropriate to instruct a bailiff, then he would probably transfer the judgment up to the High Court for enforcement. The process is started by the completion of Part 1 of Form N293A. This form is shown at the end of this Chapter.

When completing N293A, you should provide the judgment details and attach a copy of the sealed judgment or order. The form should be signed by the creditor or their solicitor. This completed form is then sent (or taken) to the County Court that issued the judgment. Providing everything is in order and the judgment still stands, then the court will seal Part 2 of the Form N293A, authorising the transfer to the High Court for the purposes of enforcement. The Judgment however remains a County Court judgment.

Once the Form N293A has been sealed, it is returned and can then be submitted to the High Court or a local District Registry (a High Court section within many County Courts) with a completed Form 53 writ of control. An example of a completed writ of control is shown below at the end of this Chapter. There is a court fee (currently £60) which must be paid at the same time the two forms are submitted. The fee is paid to HMCTS (Her Majesty's Courts and Tribunals Service) and is non-refundable. However, the fee is added to the sum to be recovered from the debtor. The High Court or District Registry will check the details of the forms and, providing everything is in order, will seal the Writ of Control accordingly.

The creditor does not have to concern himself with the paperwork for transferring up the CCJ to the High Court as all High Court Enforcement companies will do this for the creditor at no cost (i.e. only require the payment of the court fee to transfer up). All the creditor has to do is send the High Court Enforcement company a copy of the County Court Judgment and the court fee and the High Court Enforcement company will do the rest.

As to which High Court Enforcement Company to select, it is probably best to seek a recommendation from someone you trust. Also, when contacting the various companies in the sector, you may wish to ask what areas of the country they cover.

****

Combined certificate of judgment and request for writ of control or writ of possession

In the	
Claim No.	
Creditor's/ Claimant's Ref.	
Debtor's/ Defendant's Ref.	
Date	

Creditor/Claimant

Debtor/Defendant

I certify that the details I have given are correct and that to my knowledge there is no application or other procedure pending.

I request an order for enforcement in the High Court by

☐ Writ of Control

☐ Writ of Possession

I intend to enforce the judgment or order by execution against goods, and/or against trespassers in the High Court and require this Certificate for this purpose.

....
signed - (Creditor/Creditor's legal representative)
(Claimant/Claimant's legal representative)

....date

Part 1

Date of judgment or order

Total amount of judgment
including any costs

or

Details of order for possession
including any costs

Total amount of interest accrued at the rate of [   ] per day to date *(if any)*

Part 2 *(for court use only)*

I certify that this is a true extract of the court record in this case.

Order for enforcement in the High Court by

☐ Writ of Control

☐ Writ of Possession

made on (date)...

....An Officer of the Court

(Seal)

Please Note:

This judgment or order has been sent to the High Court for enforcement by (Writ of Control) (Writ of Possession against trespassers) only.

The county court claim has not been transferred to the High Court. Applications for other methods of enforcement or ancillary applications must be made to the County Court hearing centre in which the judgment or order was made, unless the case has since been transferred to a different court, in which case it must be made to that court.

For further details of the courts www.gov.uk/find-court-tribunal. When corresponding with the Court, please address forms or letters to the Manager and always quote the claim number.

THE ACTION DEPARTMENT of the High Court is open between 10am and 4.30pm. All correspondence should be sent to the Court Manager, Action Department, Royal Courts of Justice, Strand, London WC2A 2LL

N293A Combined certificate of judgment and request for writ of fieri facias or writ of possession (04.14)   *I continued overleaf*

Part 3

In the High Court of Justice

Queen's Bench Division at

(Sent from the   County Court by

Certificate dated the   day of   )

High Court Enforcement Number

County Court Claim Number

Address of (Debtor)
(property of which possession is to be given)

Seal a Writ of (Control)(Possession) directed to the:

To: "_____, an enforcement officer authorised to enforce writs of execution from the High Court'.

Or,

'The enforcement officers authorised to enforce writs of execution from the High Court who are assigned to the district of ¹ _____ in England and Wales'.

Note: If you have chosen this option you must send this writ to the National Information Centre for Enforcement for allocation.

against [_____]

for: *(Complete A, B, C as appropriate)*

A. the sum of:

    (a) debt   £

    (b) costs and interest   £

    (c) Subsequent costs   £

    (if any)

B. and interest thereon at ....% per annum from the date of transfer and costs of execution

C. possession of [_____]

and £[_____] for costs.

Signed
Address for service
Date

20

No. 53 - Writ of Control

In the High Court of Justice
Queen's Division
Newtown District Registry
County Court Claim No.
AB04YU12

Jeff Appleyard	**Claimant**
Fred Smith	**Defendant**

ELIZABETH THE SECOND, by the Grace of God, of the United Kingdom of Great Britain and Northern Ireland and of Our other realms and territories Queen, Head of the Commonwealth, Defender of the Faith.

TO: *Joe Wilson an enforcement officer authorised to enforce writs of control issued from the High Court.*

IN THIS CLAIM a Judgment or Order was made as set out in the Schedule.

YOU ARE NOW COMMANDED to take control of the goods of the defendant authorised by law and raise therefrom the sums detailed in the Schedule, together with fees and charges to which you are entitled. And immediately after execution pay the claimant the said sums and interest.

YOU ARE ALSO COMMANDED to indorse on this writ immediately after taking control of goods a statement of the manner in which you have done so and send a copy of the statement to the

THIS WRIT WAS ISSUED by the Newtown District Registry of the High Court on 1 Sept 2015 on the application of Jeff Appleyard of 10 Downend Road, Newtown , NT10 3DR the claimant

WITNESS The Right Honourable Michael Gove MP Lord High Chancellor of Great Britain

The address for enforcement are 40 Bighouse Manor, Newtown, NW10 3ER.

SCHEDULE

1. Date of Judgment or Order: 1 May 2015	
2. Amount of Judgment or Order (including interest awarded by Judgment or Order)	£15,000
3. Fixed costs on Judgment or Order	£750.00
4. Assessed costs (if any) [by costs certificate dated (date)]	£
5. (If sent from County Court by certificate) Interest[1] post-Judgment or Order on County Court judgment or order over £5,000) until date of certificate	£
6. **LESS** credits or payments received since Judgment or Order	£
Sub Total	£
7. Fixed costs on issue	£111.75
Total	**£15,861.75**

Together with: -

A. Judgment interest[2] at 8% from date of Judgment on sub-total above, or (if sent from County Court by certificate) date of County Court certificate on paragraphs 1,2 and 3 above until payment,

B. Fees and Charges to which you are entitled (where appropriate).

Creditors' Responsibilities

5. In order for the enforcement process to work effectively, creditors must be fully aware of their own responsibilities. The primary purpose of this guidance for creditors is to draw their attention to their responsibilities when instructing and dealing with enforcement agents/agencies to recover debts on their behalf.

6. The creditors responsibilities should be observed and set out in terms of agreement with their enforcement agent/agency. They should consider carefully any specific requirements for financial guarantees so that these are adequate, fair and appropriate for the work involved.

7. Creditors should remember that enforcement agents are acting on their behalf and that ultimately they are responsible, and accountable, for the enforcement agents acting on their behalf.

8. Creditors should act proportionately when seeking to recover debt, taking into account debtors' circumstances.

9. Creditors must notify the enforcement agency of all payments received and other contacts with the debtor, including repayment agreements made with the debtor.

10. Creditors have a responsibility to tell the debtor that if payment is not made within a specified period of time, action may be taken to enforce payment.

11. Creditors agreeing the suspension of a warrant or making direct payment arrangements with debtors must give appropriate notification to and should pay appropriate fees due to the enforcement agent for the work they have undertaken.

12. Creditors must not issue a warrant knowing that the debtor is not at the address, as a means of tracing the debtor at no cost.

13. Creditors must provide a contact point at appropriate times to enable the enforcement agent or agency to make essential queries, particularly where they have cause for concern.

14. Creditors must consider the appropriateness of referring debtors in potentially vulnerable situations to enforcement agents and, if they choose to proceed, must alert the enforcement agent to this situation.

15. Creditors should ensure that there are clear protocols agreed with their enforcement agents governing the approach that should be taken when a debtor has been identified as vulnerable.

16. Should a debtor be identified as vulnerable, creditors should be prepared to take control of the case, at any time, if necessary.

17. Creditors should inform the enforcement agency if they have any cause to believe that the debtor may present a risk to the safety of the enforcement agent.

18. Creditors should have a clear complaints procedure in place to address complaints regarding their own enforcement agents or external enforcement agents acting on their behalf.

Request for Warrant of Control
to be completed and signed by the creditor or their legal representative and sent to the court with the appropriate fee.

1. Creditor's name and address	**In the**
	Claim no.
	Fee Account no.

2. Name and address for service and payment (if different from above) Ref/Tel No.	for court use only
	Warrant no.
	Issue date:
	Warrant applied for at o'clock
3. Debtor's name and address	Court code:

4. Warrant details

(A) Balance due at date of this request	
(B) Amount for which warrant to issue	
Issue fee	
Legal representative's costs	
Land Registry fee	
TOTAL	

If the amount of the warrant at (B) is less than the balance at (A), the sum due after the warrant is paid will be

I certify that the whole or part of any instalments due under the judgment or order have not been paid and the balance now due is as shown

Signed

Creditor (Creditor's legal representative)

Dated

IMPORTANT
You must inform the court immediately of any payments you receive after you have sent this request to the court

You should provide a contact number so that the bailiff can speak to you if they need to:
Daytime phone number: Evening phone number *(if possible)*:
Contact name *(where appropriate)*:
Debtor's phone number *(if known)*:

If you have any other information which may help the bailiff or if you have reason to believe that the bailiff may encounter any difficulties you should write it below.

Part 2

Giving Notice

Before an Enforcement Officer can attend to try and collect this £4,000 debt, there is a requirement that Notice of not less than 7 clear days must be given to the Judgment Debtor. This Notice must be given by the Enforcement Agent and not the Creditor. Sundays, Bank Holidays, Good Friday and Christmas Day do not count when calculating this period of time. The Notice must contain certain prescribed information. A copy of the Notice in its prescribed form is shown at the end of this Chapter.

Upon the giving of Notice of the intention to take control of goods, in law at that point the goods cannot be assigned or transferred by the debtor. In legal terminology, it means that the goods become "bound". In simple terms, this means that unless the person who acquired the goods of the debtor did so in good faith, for valuable consideration and without knowing about a warrant, then the transfer or sale of the item will not be considered valid and accordingly the goods can be seized by the enforcement agent. Valuable consideration means that the buyer gives the debtor something of economic value (e.g. money) in returns for the goods, rather than the debtor simply transferring the items to the purchaser.

It is not an uncommon situation for debtors to attempt to 'sell' (or transfer) goods to a friend, partner or relative after receiving correspondence or a visit from a bailiff. In reality, it would be difficult for a bailiff to know whether you've given away belongings before they visit your home or business premises. However, if the bailiff suspects you have given goods away, they can apply for permission from the court to enter the premises where they believe your goods are being kept or stored. This could mean that giving away goods to hide them from the bailiffs is actually more trouble than it's worth.

Example:

Mr Fred Jones has a County Court judgment against him for the sum of £10,000. The creditor, Mr John Snell, applies to transfer the judgment up to the High Court by a High Court enforcement officer. A notice of intention to take control of goods is served on Mr Fred Jones and three days after receiving the notice, Mr Jones transfers his only valuable asset (a Jaguar motor vehicle worth £15,000) to his girlfriend Sharon. Mr Jones says to his girlfriend that he needs to transfer the car as he has Bailiffs after him. In this case, it is likely that Sharon would not have acquired title to the Jaguar in good faith.

Does a residential tenant receive notice of the eviction date where the possession is carried out by a High Court Enforcement Officer?

The giving of Notice before an enforcement agent attends to take control of goods does not apply to a High Court Enforcement Officer attending to enforce a possession order in a residential tenancy situation. Readers may have seen television programmes about High Court Enforcement Officers who attend to take possession of a property without the date of the eviction being given to the tenant. Notice of the eviction date will be given where it is being carried out by a county court bailiff. However, a High Court Enforcement Officer can carry out an eviction of a residential tenant without giving notice of the eviction date. If a landlord wishes to transfer up the possession order to the High Court, he must seek permission from the Court for the transfer and permission for the issue of a writ of possession by the High Court. Notice of the application for these permissions must be given to the tenant, but once the warrant is issued the actual date of the eviction does not have to be given in advance by the High Court Enforcement Officers. Transferring up to the High Court might be cost effective for a Landlord where the rent is high and the waiting time for a county court bailiff might be 6 to 8 weeks. To Transfer a Mortgage Possession Order or an Order for Possession against trespassers to the High Court does not require permission.

The permission to transfer can be asked for in the Claim Form or after the possession order is granted by making an application seeking permission to transfer up to the High Court for enforcement by a High Court Enforcement Officer. The Court Rules (CPR Part 83.13) require that the Notice of the application for permission must be given to the occupants of the property. When seeking permission, reasons need to be given as to why you want to transfer up to the High Court for enforcement.

In the case of **Birmingham City Council v. Mondhlani (6 November 2015)**, District Judge Salmon made detailed comments about the process for transferring a possession order to the High Court for enforcement. The Judge made it clear that not only is there a need for an application to transfer up to the High Court but there was also a requirement to apply to the High Court for permission to issue a writ of possession in the High Court. It was also made clear that the tenant must receive notice of the application. The Judge saw no reason why the applications for transfer and permission to issue a writ of possession could not be made at the same time provided the requisite notice was given to all occupiers of the application. It was also noted that the High Court Enforcement Officer does not have to give notice of the eviction date to the tenant.

The case of **Birmingham City Council v. Mondhlani** is of significance because the judge set out the factors which a court should take into account when considering giving permission to transfer up a possession order to the High Court. It was stated that the County Court orders are normally enforced in the County Court and so the burden is on the applicants for a transfer to show why the case would be transferred up to the High Court for enforcement. The applicant needs to show some significant advantage for having the case transferred up. This could be in terms of cost and speed. The judge stated that it is important to ensure that a transfer to the High Court does not unfairly prejudice tenants. However, because the process is quicker it does not necessarily amount to prejudice provided the tenant has had an opportunity to set aside the writ of possession. The court must also consider the impact of any transfer on court resources and the impact on other cases. The fact that the writ might be suspended by the court is a relevant factor to be considered when transferring the order to the High Court.

In the case of **Birmingham City Council v. Mondhlani** the Judge considered the advantages of a transfer and the prejudice that may be caused to the tenant. The argument often put forward in favour of a transfer up is that it would save time. However, in this case it was suggested that the time advantages may not be as great as first thought. After the transfer it cannot simply apply for and obtain a writ of possession administratively; the process of making an application to the High Court for permission to issue a writ of possession takes time and court resources. Therefore, the extra steps must add in a delay.

There are advantages to the landlord in terms of having control of the writ of possession being executed in the High Court. The landlord can postpone the execution of a warrant on terms agreed with the tenant and if the terms are broken, the warrant can then simply be enforced. By contrast, in the County Court if the warrant is withdrawn because of an agreement with the tenant, then if the landlord later needs to enforce the warrant then the landlord would have to apply for the warrant to be reissued.

Using a High Court Enforcement Officer to enforce a possession order is potentially unfair prejudice to a tenant because of the greater costs of the process. In addition, it is likely that a writ of possession from the High Court will be enforced with no or minimal notice of the actual eviction date. More importantly, the tenant does not get a copy of the warrant of possession or the information contained on form N54 which in the County Court tells tenants facing eviction how they can apply to suspend the warrant of possession. In **Birmingham City Council v. Mondhlani,** the judge asked the council what steps it took after the warrant of possession was issued. Although the judge was given assurances that the tenants were given at least two weeks notice of the eviction date by letter as well as a visit by the High Court enforcement officer and information similar to that in the N54, the judge expressed his concern at the practice adopted by solicitors acting for Birmingham City Council in which the requirements of CPR 83.13(2)have been side-stepped. (CPR 83.13(2) states that a writ of possession to enforce a judgment or order for the giving of possession of any land will not be issued without the permission of the court.

The Judge identified that errors were made on the form N293A (a combined certificate of transfer up). There is wording on that form which states, *"This judgment or order has been sent to the High Court for enforcement by (Writ of Possession against trespassers) only."* As has been mentioned, permission of the Court is not required for a writ of possession to be issued against trespassers but is required where the occupiers were tenants. It was mentioned in **Birmingham City Council v. Mondhlani** that the Council had been obtaining writs of possession wrongly in that it was not making an application for permission to issue the writ of possession. The court staff relied on the inaccurately completed form N293A and were issuing writs of possession. So writs of possession were being issued in the High Court without permission, where permission was required, and so as no permission was sought the Judge was not able to check that appropriate notice had been given to the tenants. At the stage of permission being sought, the Judge stated that consideration can be given as to what safeguards need to be in place. District Judge Salmon did not state what he would expect to see in the application for permission but he felt that in almost all cases he would expect the following conditions to be in place if permission to issue a High Court writ of possession were to be given:

1. Written communication to the tenant informing them of the date of the eviction together with information in writing as to how he can apply to suspend the writ of possession and that he might be eligible for a fee remission.
2. A date for an eviction which provides for sufficient time to suspend the writ of possession.

What is the significance of the Judge's comment in Birmingham City Council v Mondhlani ?

District Judges were becoming concerned about possession orders being transferred up to the High Court without proper notice and the writ of possession being issued without permission, as well as the eviction being carried out without any notice to the tenant of the date. Although a High Court writ of possession can be enforced without giving notice of the date of the eviction, there are safeguards which the court will expect to see in the application for transfer/permission. This means that for a Judge to agree to transfer and grant permission for a High Court writ of possession to be issued, the landlord is going to have satisfy the Judge that notice of the eviction date will be given. It is likely that fewer transfers up to the High Court will be granted because Judges will scrutinise more thoroughly the applications. This will provide a degree of relief to tenants who have High Court Enforcements Officers turning up to carry out an eviction without any warning of the date.

If a tenant, who has been taken to court by the landlord to recover possession, receives a notice that permission is being sought to transfer up the possession order from the County Court to the High Court, then the tenant should act quickly and seek advice if they want to try and suspend the eviction. If they don't act quickly, the next thing that will happen, if permission is granted for the transfer and the issue of a High Court writ of possession, is that they will received a visit from the High Court Enforcement Officer without any warning to carry out the eviction.

It has been mentioned by legal commentators that there is the possibility that writs of possession were being issued in the High Court without an application for permission having been made. It might be that some of the evictions were unlawful.

How is the Notice Given?

The Notice can be given to the Debtor in one of the following ways:

- By Post
- By Fax

- By Hand
- By fixing the Notice at or in a place where it is likely to come the attention of the debtor
- By handing it personally to the debtor.

If the debtor is not an individual, e.g. a company, the Notice can be delivered to the place of business or registered office of the company.

Smith v. Household Supplies Ltd

Mr Smith lives at 10 Marden Road, Downton. He has built up debts and one of his creditors, Household Supplies Ltd obtained a county court judgment against him for the sum of £4,000. Household transferred the judgment up to the High Court for Enforcement by a High Court Enforcement Officer. High Court Collections were passed the warrant of control to enforce. They send out a Notice to Mr Smith on Monday 6th September. On Friday 10 September, the enforcement officer Fred Jones attends 10 Marden Road to attempt to take control of goods. Fred arrives to find a door open and so he is able to make a peaceful entry and takes control of goods inside including a new large flat screen television and a surround sound cinema player.

In the case of Smith Household Supplies Ltd, there is a defect in the giving of Notice. There was not 7 clear days between the date of giving the Notice and the date the Enforcement agent attended to take control of goods.

Once the Notice requirement has been complied with, the Enforcement Agent may attend to try and take control of goods.

Notice of enforcement

This notice must be given by the enforcement agent or the enforcement agent's office.

Please read this notice - it is important

Name of Debtor

Address

Date notice issued ☐☐ / ☐☐ / ☐☐☐☐

Enforcement agent reference number

About this notice You have been sent this notice of enforcement because you have not paid money that you owe.

Who you owe money to

The amount you owe them

Their ref./account no. (if applicable)

Enforcement details Details of the court judgment or order or enforcement power by virtue of which the debt is enforceable

Sum outstanding

Debt

Interest

Compliance stage fee

TOTAL sum outstanding

(as at the date of this notice)

When to make payment	You must pay, or agree a payment arrangement with the enforcement agent, by:

Date ☐☐ / ☐☐ / ☐☐☐☐

Time ☐

If you do not pay   If you do not pay or agree a payment arrangement by the date above, an enforcement agent will visit you and may seize your belongings - this is called 'taking control'. These belongings may then be sold to pay the money you owe. These actions will increase the costs of enforcement and these costs will be added to the amount already owed.

Possible additional fees and expenses of enforcement   If the sum outstanding remains unpaid or you have not agreed a payment arrangement by the date and time above you may be charged the following (enforcement agent to detail further possible fees and expenses)

How to pay what you owe   How to pay including opening hours and days

How you can contact the enforcement agent or the enforcement agent's office

Telephone ☐

Address ☐

Opening hours and days ☐

You can seek free advice and information from

AdviceUK at www.adviceuk.org.uk/find-a-member

National Debtline at www.nationaldebtline.org or 0808 808 4000

Money Advice Service at www.moneyadviceservice.org.uk or on 0300 500 5000

Gov.uk at www.gov.uk

Other free advice is available.

35

Part 3

Preventing and postponing a warrant

If a debtor is faced with an enforcement agent giving Notice to attend to enforce a warrant of control there is the opportunity to apply to the court to try and stay or postpone its enforcement. The High Court has the power under section 70 of the Tribunals Courts and Enforcement Act 2007 to order stays. Section 70 reads:

(1) If, at any time, the High Court is satisfied that a party to proceedings is unable to pay—
(a) a sum recovered against him (by way of satisfaction of the claim or counterclaim in the proceedings or by way of costs or otherwise), or
(b) any instalment of such a sum, the court may stay the execution of any writ of control issued in the proceedings, for whatever period and on whatever terms it thinks fit.
(2) The court may act under subsection (1) from time to time until it appears that the cause of the inability to pay has ceased.

The debtor must apply to the court on form N244 for a stay of execution. The application should contain a witness statement to show that the party is unable to pay. An example of when a debtor may seek to apply to stay the enforcement is that he does not have the ability to pay but can pay by instalments or at a particular time in the future when funds become available. An example of such an application is set out at the end this Chapter.

The Court has broad discretion to stay execution but it will usually only deprive a claimant of the opportunity to immediately enforce its judgment if there is a good reason.

Postponing a warrant of possession

If a tenant receives a possession order or a notice of the application to transfer to the High Court for the possession order to be enforced by a High Court enforcement officer, they must act quickly if they want to seek a stay of eviction presuming they have grounds for doing so. An application for a stay should be made immediately to the court.

Let's suppose that a landlord has obtained a possession order on discretionary grounds, which is where the judge is not obliged to grant possession; in such a case, the judge not only has to be satisfied that the grounds for seeking possession are proved but also that it is reasonable in all the circumstances to grant possession.

A mandatory ground for possession is where the judge must award possession if the ground is established. For example, if a landlord serves a section 8 notice seeking possession of an assured tenancy on grounds of rent arrears, and the rent is at least two months in arrears at the time of serving the notice and there are two months rent arrears at the time court proceedings are commenced, then if there are at least two months arrears at the hearing the judge has no option but to grant possession. A "Section 8 notice" is named after section 8 of the Housing Act 1988 (as amended). Under this section, a landlord can give formal legal notice that he intends to seek possession on certain specified grounds (such as rent arrears or other breaches of the tenancy) as stated in the Housing Act 1988.

If the rent at the service of the section 8 notice is only one month in arrears and when proceedings start the rent is two months in arrears and three months in arrears at the hearing, the judge has discretion not to grant a possession order. In such an example, suppose the tenant does not attend the hearing and the judge grants a possession order (as is quite often the case) then on receipt of the possession order the tenant might seek to apply for a stay of possession if they can establish grounds to persuade a judge to do so.

Let us suppose the reason the tenant did not attend the hearing was that he was in hospital and a few days after the hearing he leaves hospital and discovers the possession order was made on a discretionary ground. He immediately makes an application to stay the possession order and at the same time clears a large portion of the rent arrears and states that the remaining arrears will be paid within 14 days. There is a reasonable possibility that the judge might order a stay on the basis that the arrears are cleared in the way put forward by the tenant.

Set out below is an example of what the tenant might say on the Application Notice to the Court when he/she applies for a stay of a warrant of possession.

Suspending Warrants issued by a Magistrates Court

There is less understanding as to how and whether magistrates can suspend a warrant. Once a warrant of control has been issued by a Magistrates Court, you generally can't apply for it to be withdrawn. Magistrates' courts have no power to postpone or delay bailiff action once a warrant has been issued, except in very exceptional circumstances, for example if they agree you are a vulnerable person.

If a warrant of control has been issued by a Magistrates Court and you are seeking to vary the payments because of a change in financial circumstances, then you could contact the fines officer at the court in writing and ask for the court to vary or remit the fine. The debtor can then expect a means enquiry into their financial circumstances to be conducted.

There may be situations where a Magistrates Court has issued a warrant without the Defendant receiving Notice of the proceedings and the first that they know of the matter is when they receive a Notice of Enforcement or a bailiff arrives representing Marston Group, Collectica Ltd, Excel Enforcement or Swift; these are the four certified bailiff companies that are contracted to collect Magistrates Courts fines. Under section 14 of the Magistrates' Courts Act 1980, proceedings which begin with a summons or requisition will become void if the defendant, at any time during or after the trial, makes a Statutory Declaration that he or she did not know of the proceedings until a date after the trial began. In order to make the Statutory Declaration, you can either make the

Statutory Declaration in writing and submit it to the court or you can ask the court to list a hearing for you to make your statutory declaration in person at the court. The form of Statutory Declaration is set out at the end of this Chapter. The Statutory Declaration must be served on the court within 21 days after finding out about the case. If you serve the Statutory Declaration after 21 days of finding out about the case then you must provide a reason for the delay.

How long does a warrant remain valid for ?

An enforcement agent has a period of 12 months from the date of the Notice of Enforcement in which to take control of the debtors goods. It is not uncommon that the debtor will contact the bailiff upon receipt of the Notice of Enforcement to agree a repayment plan. If that happens, and the repayment plan is breached the period of 12 months will run from the date of the breach and not the date of the Notice. This is set out in Regulation 9 of the Taking Control of Goods Regulations 2013. If the period of 12 months is going to expire then under this Regulation the bailiff or the creditor can apply for an extension of up to 12 months.

****

Application notice

For help in completing this form please read the notes for guidance form N244Notes.

In the	UPTON DISTRICT REGISTRY OF THE HIGH COURT
Claim no.	UP123WQ12
Fee Account no.	
Warrant no. (if applicable)	AP1000098
Claimant's name (including ref.)	Phones and Gadgets R Us Ltd
Defendant's name (including ref.)	Brian Parker
Date	xx/xx/xx

1. What is your name or, if you are a legal representative, the name of your firm?

2. Are you a ☐ Claimant ☑ Defendant ☐ Legal Representative

   ☐ Other *(please specify)*

   If you are a legal representative whom do you represent?

3. What order are you asking the court to make and why?

   I am seeking a stay of enforcement of the writ of control under section 70 of the Tribunals Courts and Enforcement Act 2007 because I am currently unable to pay

4. Have you attached a draft of the order you are applying for? ☑ Yes ☐ No

5. How do you want to have this application dealt with? ☑ at a hearing ☐ without a hearing

   ☐ at a telephone hearing

6. How long do you think the hearing will last? [ ] Hours 10 Minutes

   Is this time estimate agreed by all parties? ☐ Yes ☑ No

7. Give details of any fixed trial date or period

   None

8. What level of Judge does your hearing need?

   District Judge

9. Who should be served with this application?

   Claimant and Care Free Bailiffs Ltd

9a. Please give the service address, (other than details of the claimant or defendant) of any party named in question 9.

   Carefree Bailiffs Ltd
   10 market Road
   Upton
   U23 8YT

41

10. What information will you be relying on, in support of your application?

☐ the attached witness statement

☐ the statement of case

☑ the evidence set out in the box below

If necessary, please continue on a separate sheet.

1. I am currently unable to make payment of the amount due under the warrant of control. As can be seen by the attached statement of my income and expenditure, I have only £25 per month disposable income. However, I am due to receive a pay out in respect of an accident claim and I will use the compensation to settle in full this debt. I attach documentary evidence that I will be receiving this lump sum payment on the xx/xx/xx.

2. I therefore ask the Court to stay the enforcement for a period of two months to allow me to receive the compensation payment and pay it over to the Claimant to settle the debt.

Statement of Truth

(I believe) (The applicant believes) that the facts stated in this section (and any continuation sheets) are true.

Signed _____ Dated _____

Applicant('s legal representative)('s litigation friend)

Full name   BRIAN PARKER

Name of applicant's legal representative's firm _____

Position or office held _____
(if signing on behalf of firm or company)

---

11. Signature and address details

Signed _____ Dated _____

Applicant('s legal representative's)('s litigation friend)

Position or office held   BRIAN PARKER

(if signing on behalf of firm or company)

Applicant's address to which documents about this application should be sent

130 Rose Avenue UPTON		If applicable	
	Phone no.	01377 000123	
	Fax no.		
	DX no.		
Postcode U P 1 2 4 L L	Ref no.		

E-mail address	

42

STATUTORY DECLARATION

(Criminal Procedure Rules, rule 37.16; Magistrates' Courts Act 1980, section 14)

Original Case Number:	Account reference number:	New Case number:
▓	▓	▓

Case details

Defendant's full name: ▓
Current address: ▓
Defendant's date of birth: ▓
Convicted at:
This declaration was made at: ▓ Magistrates' Court
                                 ▓ Magistrates' Court, or
                                 ▓ address of solicitor or Commissioner for Oaths

Declaration

I do solemnly and sincerely declare that:

1. I am the defendant named above.
2. I now know that the hearing in this case began on or about ▓ *(date).*
3. I found out about the case on ▓ *(date)* because: *Explain briefly how you found out. If you use an electronic version of this form, the space beneath will expand.*[1] *If you use a paper version and need more space, use the back of the form.* ▓

And I make this solemn declaration conscientiously believing it to be true, under the provisions of the Statutory Declarations Act 1835.

WARNING. Under section 5 of the Perjury Act 1911, if you knowingly and wilfully make a statutory declaration that is false in a material particular, then you are guilty of an offence, and liable on conviction to a term of imprisonment for up to 2 years, or to a fine, or both.

Signed: .... *(defendant)*

Date: ▓

Declared before me :

Signed: ....

Name: ▓   [Magistrate]
                                   [District Judge (Magistrates' Court)]
                                   [Solicitor / Commissioner for Oaths]

Extension of time to deliver this declaration

The time limit for delivering this declaration to the court office for the magistrates' court where the trial took place is **21 days** from the date you found out about the case. If you have taken longer than that to deliver it to that court office, explain why here. *If you use an electronic version of this form, the space beneath will expand. If you use a paper version and need more space, use the back of this form.*

▓

For use by the court if allowing an extension of time:

I extended the time for delivering this declaration because: *Give brief reasons.* ▓

Signed: ....

Name: ▓   [Magistrate]
Date: ▓   [District Judge (Magistrates' Court)]
                                   [Justices' Clerk / Assistant Clerk]

---

[1] Forms for use with the Rules are at: http://www.justice.gov.uk/courts/procedure-rules/criminal/formspage.

How to use this form

1. Complete the case details box and the declaration above.

2. Make the declaration before a magistrate, a District Judge (Magistrates' Courts), or a solicitor or Commissioner for Oaths. You can ask for help at any magistrates' court office. See also the notes for guidance beneath.

4. Send or deliver the completed declaration to the court office for the magistrates' court where the trial took place. They must receive it not more than 21 days after you found out about the case. The court may extend that time limit, but if your declaration is late you must explain why in the box above.

Notes for Guidance

Under section 14 of the Magistrates' Courts Act 1980, a trial is void where:

- the case started with a summons or requisition,
- the defendant did not know about the case, and
- not more than 21 days after finding out about it (which time limit can be extended) the defendant delivers to the court a statutory declaration that he or she did not know about the case until after the trial.

A fresh trial must be by different magistrates. The result of a fresh trial may be different to the result of the first trial, or it may be the same.

Under the Statutory Declarations Act 1835, the defendant's declaration can be made before anyone who is authorised by law to hear it (e.g. a solicitor), or before any Justice of the Peace (a magistrate or District Judge (Magistrates' Courts). The person who hears the declaration need not enquire into the truth of it. That person's function is limited to hearing the declaration, and certifying that he or she has done so by signing it. If the declaration turns out to be untrue, the defendant making it may be punished for perjury.

How you found out about the case
Why this declaration is late

If you need extra space, continue your explanation(s) here from the front of this form.

Note for court staff

If this declaration is made at a court, any available record of the conviction should be submitted to the magistrate or District Judge (Magistrates' Court) before whom it is made.

If the court directs that the case be relisted at once for a fresh trial, enter the hearing date:

January 2015

44

Part 4

The bailiff arrives

If a bailiff has arrived at their door it is usually because the debtor has refused to pay or they have not got the funds to pay. This may sound obvious but those who say it is a complete surprise that a bailiff is knocking on the door are often not being truthful. There will of course be situations where people have not had any notice of proceedings but those are rare. In view of the various pre-action correspondence that is required before taking legal action, the sending of the court papers to obtain a court judgment, as well as the enforcement notice that a bailiff has to send, the chances of a debtor not knowing anything about the unpaid amount are rather rare. There are occasions when a judgment is obtained by sending paperwork to a previous address of the debtor. In such a case, the debtor may not have notice of the court action and the judgment, although in an age of people receiving updates whenever something impacts on their credit file, this will probably happen less often.

When the knock on the door comes, the debtor should, and is perfectly entitled to, check the identity of the person purporting to be a bailiff with powers to enforce a court judgment or fine. In view of the big increase in court fees recently, it is possible that some organisations will instruct those who are not actually "bailiffs" but are "debt collectors" who have come visiting to try and persuade you to make payments. These "debt collectors" do not have the powers of actual bailiffs (be they High Court Enforcement Officers, County Court Bailiffs or Certified bailiffs.)

When faced with a bailiff at your door, or someone claiming to be a bailiff, it is sensible to take reasonable measures to check their identity and the authority they have. You ask to see;

- Proof of their identity (such as ID badge or their enforcement agent certificate)
- Which company they are from
- A telephone number

To check the bailiff's identity, you will need to ask (find out from their identity card) the type of bailiff they are. You could then go on-line and check the register of certificated bailiff at:

http://certificatedbailiffs.justice.gov.uk/CertificatedBailiffs/

If they say they are a high court enforcement officer, then you could check the list at:

http://www.hceoa.org.uk/members/authorised-members-directory.html

Now obviously it might be difficult when faced with a bailiff at your door to calmly decide to say that you want to take time to check their identity but that is the sensible thing to do if you have any doubts. Indeed, if the bailiff is who he claims to be then they should not have an issue with this. The National Standards for Taking

46

Control of Goods which bailiffs must adhere to states at paragraph 22 that:

22. Enforcement agents should always produce relevant identification to the debtor, such as a badge or ID card, together with any written authorisation to act on behalf of the creditor (in appropriate debt types).

If the person on the doorstep starts to get agitated or aggressive then this might raise your suspicions. The National Standards at paragraph 21 says:

21. Enforcement agents must not act in a threatening manner when visiting the debtor by making gestures or taking actions which could reasonably be construed as suggesting harm or risk of harm to debtors, their families, appointed third parties or property.

So a genuine enforcement agent/bailiff is unlikely to act in such a manner because if he does so, then he/she leaves themselves open to a complaint and action that threaten their certification and ultimately their livelihood. That is not to say that genuine bailiffs would never act in such a way but it is unlikely for a professional person to behave in a such a way and thus jeopardise their career.

When bailiffs are at the door of the premises it usually prompts a whole host of questions from debtors and creditors as to what a bailiff can or cannot do. Among the most common questions are:

1. By what means can a bailiff enter?
2. Can the bailiff use force?
3. On what day and at what times can a bailiff try and enter premises?
4. How does the bailiff actually take control of goods?

5. What items is the bailiff allowed to take control of and what goods are exempt?

There are potentially a multitude of questions and queries that could arise from the attendance of a bailiff but the above are some of the more common and important ones. If the bailiff does not follow the correct procedure, then the bailiff in the eyes of the law will not have validly taken control of goods.

How can the bailiff enter premises?

The new Regulations set out the means by which a bailiff can enter. It can be by any door or usual means of entry, or any usual means of entry to premises other than a building (e.g. an aircraft, ship). It is said that these rules are intended to remove some of the more unusual means of entry such as climbing in through a sky light or through an open window.

Luxury Country Hotels Limited v. Brian Haughty-Smith

Mr Haughty-Smith owes money to Luxury Country Hotels Ltd in connection with a big private party that he booked at the luxury Green Views Hotel. The party was attended by hundreds of guests and Mr Haughty-Smith was presented with a bill at the end of the event for £10,000. A dispute followed but ultimately Luxury Country Hotels obtained a judgment for this amount. They transfer the judgment up to the High Court for enforcement by a High Court Enforcement Agent. The Enforcement Agent sends a Notice of Enforcement to Mr

Haughty-Smith and 8 days after that is sent, the officer turns up at Haughty Manor to try and take control of goods. The Bailiff is faced with a locked gate at the end of a drive leading up to the house and a perimeter wall circling the whole of Haughty Manor. The perimeter wall is 5 foot high and the bailiff, Fred Jones, has no difficulty in placing a ladder against the wall and climbing over it. Fred walks up the driveway and finds an expensive Lamborghini car parked in front of the house. The bailiff is aware from information provided to him by the Luxury Country Hotels that this vehicle is owned by Mr Haughty-Smith. Fred secures the vehicle on the premises by way of a clamp.

The question in the case of *Luxury Country Hotels* is whether the bailiff has entered the premises in a legal manor?

Before the introduction of the new Taking Control of Goods Regulation 2013, the answer to this question would have been that a bailiff could climb over a wall or a fence or walk across a garden or yard provided that no damage occurs. This was established in the case of **Long v Clarke & another [1894] 1 QB 119.** However, section 65 of the Tribunal Courts and Enforcement Act 2007 states that the common law rules are replaced by the procedure in Schedule 12 of the Act. Taking Control of Goods Regulations 2013 was introduced to supplement Part 3 of the Tribunals, Courts and Enforcement Act 2007 which is concerned with the taking control of goods. The Regulations make detailed provision for the operation of the procedure in Schedule 12 which enforcement agents must follow when taking control of goods and selling them to recover a sum of money. Regulation 20 states:

Mode of entry or re-entry to premises

20. The enforcement agent may enter relevant or specified premises under paragraph 14 or 15 of Schedule 12 respectively, or re-enter premises under paragraph 16 of Schedule 12, only by—

(a)any door, or any usual means by which entry is gained to the premises (for example, a loading bay to premises where a trade or business is carried on); or

(b)any usual means of entry, where the premises are a vehicle, vessel, aircraft, hovercraft, a tent or other moveable structure

As the Regulations refer to "usual means of entry", it is likely that climbing over a wall or boundary fence (however small) would not be regarded as entry by usual means. It also appears to prevent the climbing over a locked gate in the perimeter of premises. This will cause more problems for bailiffs in seeking to gain entry to premises. So in the case of **Brian Haughty-Smith** it can be argued that Fred Jones the bailiff has not entered the premises by a door or a usual means making the entry illegal. To be absolutely sure on this interpretation of Regulation 20, we would have to wait for a court decision on this point. The problem is that we could wait a long time for such a case.

Can the bailiff use force to gain entry?

This always seems to be the key question posed by debtors; that is understandable by debtors who simply want to avoid a bailiff successfully taking goods away. The answer depends on the nature of the warrant and whether the bailiff is recovering debts against a business. Force can be used to gain entry without a warrant where the bailiff is recovering court fines and civil money judgment debts where the judgment debtor is a business and it believed the debtor carries on a trade or business from the premises. However, a bailiff will be cautious about using the power.

The National Standards for Enforcement Agents (NSEA) states that the power should only be used where reasonably required and only after the debtor has been warned the power exists and of the consequences of not co-operating. Where a bailiff attends residential premises and is able to gain peaceful entry and takes control of goods under a "controlled goods agreement", if the debtor defaults on the agreement and the bailiff returns to remove goods, in those circumstances the bailiff can use force to enter residential (and business) premises to remove the goods. The power should only be used where reasonably required and after the bailiff has given notice of the intention to re-enter the premises.

Experience suggests that a bailiff will rarely be able to use force to gain entry to residential premises to recover a civil judgment debt. Debtors often wrongly believe that bailiffs can force their way into a person's home. It is apparent that if a debtor is careful, then it is not easy for a bailiff to gain entry to recover a non-commercial debt. With the new requirement to give Notice before attending, a consumer should be able to prevent a bailiff taking control of their goods by not leaving doors unlocked and not leaving goods, such as motor vehicles, parked on the highway where the bailiff can easily take control.

Using force to enter to collect criminal fines

Although a bailiff has the power to force entry when recovering criminal fines, there are guidelines set out by the Court Service. These guidelines make clear that it is the responsibility of the contractor of an enforcement agent to ensure that the forced entry power exists or if it does not exist to obtain a warrant from the court. Only certain companies are contracted to enforce magistrates court fines. No forced entry should be attempted without obtaining the prior approval of the Court Nominated Office, although responsibility for the actual forced entry will remain with the contractor.

Before approval can be given, the Manager of the enforcement company must contact the Nominated Officer at the court to explain the reasons for needing to use force and the method to be used. If approval is given then a record of it must be kept. Where approval is withheld, further dialogue should be undertaken. If the Court Nominated Officer is not available then the contractor may proceed at their own discretion. A written record of what happened must be kept.

Using force to enter having obtained a warrant

If the bailiff does not have the power to force entry without a warrant, then he must seek a warrant from the court. Warrants may be sought to enter premises or vehicles. Where the bailiff is applying to enter specified premises at which the debtor neither lives nor trades, the court may authorise the use of reasonable force to enter if it is satisfied that the application meets various conditions.

The conditions that must be met are:

- The enforcement officer is entering premises which are the debtors home or business premises or are other specified premises, <u>and</u>
- Either the bailiff is attempting to recover a tax debt or they are premises to which the goods have been deliberately removed in order to avoid them being taken into the bailiff's control, <u>and</u>
- There are likely to be goods on the premises of the debtor which control can be taken

The enforcement officer also has to explain to the court:

- The likely means of entry and the likely amount of force
- How it will leave the premises secure
- That it has regard to the sum and nature of the debt.

As many of the cases seeking a warrant to force entry will relate to a third party's premises, the court will require a high degree of proof.

Summary of when a Bailiff can force entry:

- **Collecting unpaid fines:**
  As a last resort they can force entry, whether they have been in your home before or not, if they have a Magistrates court warrant.

- **They have gained peaceful entry before:**
  If they have been into a property before by means of peaceful entry, they can then force entry when they next visit, for example, to remove good for sale which were the subject of a controlled goods agreement.

- **Entering a Commercial property:**
  Where the judgment debtor is a business and it believed the debtor carries on a trade or business from the premises. They can only do this if there is no living accommodation attached.

- **Collecting income tax or VAT:**
  They must also have permission from the court, for example a tax collector with a warrant from a Magistrates court, and they can only do this if they failed in a previous attempt at peaceful entry

- **"Following goods":**
  Where entry was gained from a different property and goods were taken into control, and they are now following the goods.

****

Notice after entry or taking control of goods (on a highway) and inventory of goods taken into control

| **Warning** | If you intentionally interfere with (for example dispose of or remove) controlled goods without a lawful excuse, you will be committing an offence and risk a fine or imprisonment. |

Please read this notice - it is important

Name of Debtor

Address

Date notice issued ☐☐ / ☐☐ / ☐☐☐☐

Enforcement agent reference number(s)

Name of enforcement agent
PRINT NAME

Enforcement details   Details of the court judgment or order or enforcement power by virtue of which the debt is enforceable

Who you owe money to

The amount you owe

Sum outstanding

Debt

Interest

Compliance stage fee

Enforcement stage fee

Expenses (if any)   Please detail the expenses

TOTAL sum outstanding

(as at the date of this notice)

55

As you have still not paid what you owe, I have, as enforcement agent, now:

Action taken   ☐ entered premises

address

  ☐ entered a vehicle on a highway with the intention of taking control of goods

Details of vehicle entered

Manufacturer	Model	Colour	Registration mark

Location of vehicle on the highway

  ☐ taken control of goods on a highway

Location on highway

When to make payment

To avoid the goods taken into control being sold payment of the sum outstanding must be paid or a payment arrangement agreed with the enforcement agent by

Date

Time

The goods will be released on payment in full (or may be released if you have agreed a payment arrangement with the enforcement agent) of the sum outstanding.

How to pay what you owe

How to pay including opening hours and days

Goods taken into control

☐ I have not taken control of any goods

☐ I have taken control of the following

Description of item (eg. Computer, television, car etc.)	Manufacturer (if known)	Model (if known)	Serial number (if known) or Registration mark if a vehicle	Material, colour and usage of the goods or any other identifying characteristics	Location and time

Signature

....

Enforcement Agent

....

PRINT NAME

If you do not pay or do not agree a payment arrangement with the enforcement agent, they may remove any goods they have taken into control to sell or secure them to sell on site. This will increase the cost of enforcement and these costs will be added to the money you owe.

You can seek free advice and information from

AdviceUK at www.adviceuk.org.uk/find-a-member

National Debtline at www.nationaldebtline.org or on 0808 808 4000

Money Advice Service at www.moneyadviceservice.org.uk or on 0300 500 5000

Gov.uk at www.gov.uk

Other free advice is available.

Part 5

When can a bailiff take control of goods?

Under the new Regulations, a bailiff can take control of goods on any day of the week. That being said, the National Standards for Enforcement Agents expect there to be respect for religion and culture and to consider the appropriateness of undertaking enforcement on a religious day or during a major culture festival. Normally control of goods can happen between 6am and 9pm, but there are exceptions to this rule:

- where the goods are on premises that are used wholly or partly for business and those premises are open for business during 9pm to 6am.
- The process of taking control of goods has started during the permitted hours and it is necessary to complete the process during the prohibited hours provided the bailiff does not remain on the premises for an unreasonable time.
- A court has made an order permitting it to take place outside the permitted hours.

Vulnerable debtors

Goods should not be taken into control where a child and/or a vulnerable person are the only persons found to be present on the premises where the goods are located. The Regulations do not give a definition of "vulnerable". Those who might be considered vulnerable include elderly people, people with disabilities, those recently bereaved, those who have difficulty in speaking or reading English. It is important for the vulnerable person to contact the enforcement agent as soon as possible to avoid a personal visit from the bailiff. The evidence that might be required to substantiate a person being vulnerable might include a letter from the DWP confirming an award of disability living allowance or a letter from their doctor.

By showing that someone is vulnerable, does not necessarily mean that a bailiff will not take any further action. In each case, they should consider the individual circumstances. Vulnerability is usually relevant in extreme cases where for example a medical condition of the vulnerable person could worsen if a bailiff visit were to take place or another example would be where an individual is unable to manage his or her own affairs. However, where the bailiff is satisfied that a person is vulnerable it will usually lead to no further visits from the bailiff and if the enforcement company is to continue with the enforcement action it is likely to be handled by someone within their organisation that is trained to deal with these situations.

If a bailiff is satisfied by the evidence of the debtor being vulnerable, the reality is that the bailiff will probably not continue with action to take control of goods. It may well be that a number of debtors will play the vulnerability card in order to avoid the bailiff taking control of their goods. However, a bailiff faced with a potentially vulnerable person will always take a cautious approach because the consequences of getting it wrong mean that it not worth taking the risk of doing the wrong thing.

The regulations provide that a vehicle which is used for transporting a disabled person will be exempt from being taken into control provided it is displaying a valid disability badge. In respect of bailiff fees, the regulations provide that if an enforcement agent identifies a person as being vulnerable on his visit to the debtor's property, he should not remove goods but instead give the debtor a chance to take advice. If the debtor does not take advice then the enforcement fee is not recoverable.

Carefree Bailiff Ltd v Mr Brian Parker

Carefree Bailiffs have been instructed to collect a debt by telecommunication company "Phones and Gadgets R US Ltd". The bailiff arrives at the premises stated on the warrant of control. The debt relates to an unpaid internet and telephone bill in the sum of £2,000. The bailiff knocks on the door and it is opened by an elderly lady (Mrs Dorothy Parker). The bailiff states that he is there in respect of the warrant. He asks if a Brian Parker lives at the address and she says, "Yes, do come in and have a glass of sherry". The bailiff enters the house and when in the hallway he asks to speak to Mr Brian Parker. The lady replies, "Brian who? But do come in have a sherry." The bailiff walks into the living room and sees valuable items and says to the lady ,"Do these belong to Mr Parker?" The elderly lady replies that everything in there belongs to Brian. The bailiff takes control of goods by locking the items in a downstairs cupboard. The bailiff leaves on the front of the cupboard door a Notice with an inventory stating that the goods have been taken into control. When Brian arrives home later that day, he is furious and takes advice regarding the action taken by the bailiff.

The issue here is whether the bailiff is in breach of Regulation 10 within Schedule 12:

Circumstances in which the enforcement agent may not take control of goods:
10.—(1) The enforcement agent may not take control of goods of the debtor where—

(a)the debtor is a child;

(b)a child or vulnerable person (whether more than one or a combination of both) is the only person present in the relevant or specified premises in which the goods are located; or

(c)the goods are also premises in which a child or vulnerable person (whether more than one or a combination of both) is the only person present.

(2) Where an item which belongs to the debtor is in use by any person at the time at which the enforcement agent seeks to take control of it, the enforcement agent may not do so if such action is in all the circumstances likely to result in a breach of the peace.

(3) In paragraph (2), "in use" means that the item is in the hands of, or being operated by, the person.

As can be seen, an enforcement agent must not take control of goods where the only person on the premises is a vulnerable person. It would appear that Mrs Dorothy Parker is a vulnerable person. Although there is no specific definition of "vulnerable", the facts of this case would suggest that she is vulnerable because she appears to be confused. Therefore, in such circumstances it would be wrong for a bailiff to take advantage of her vulnerability. At the end of this Chapter is the Application that Mr Parker could make to the Court in this case.

While most reasonable people would want bailiffs to treat vulnerable people with additional care, there will be those debtors who will take advantage of the bailiff's understandable hesitation when he encounters what on the face of things is a vulnerable person. I have come across situations where clearly the debtor is "playing the vulnerability card" but the bailiffs took a cautious approach and allowed the debtor to avoid enforcement action and decided in the circumstances not to seize the debtor's vehicle.

What is taking control of Goods? How is it done?

The process of taking control of goods is achieved by the bailiff doing one of the following things:

- securing the goods on the premises on which he finds them
- securing the goods on a highway (there is a distinction between vehicles and other goods found on a road).
- removing them and securing them elsewhere
- entering into a controlled goods agreement with the debtor.

If a bailiff fails to take goods into control by one of the prescribed methods then the goods would not have been taken into control. It would be a breach of the TCE Act 2007 and could lead to a claim for damages.

On premises:

The Regulations provide detailed guidance on the manner of securing goods on debtor's premises. In general, goods may be secured:

- in a cupboard, room, garage or outbuilding
- by fitting an immobilisation device
- on premises used solely for business purposes by leaving a bailiff to guard the goods taken into control.
- By locking up the premises

The first three of the above may not be used if it would deprive any person in occupation from having access to essential services such as a kitchen or bathroom. Entry and exit to the premises should not be restricted in any way and fire escapes should be kept clear.

On a Highway:

A bailiff may secure goods found on a highway where they are discovered or nearby. A highway is not defined in the TCE Act 2007 but it is regarded as having a wide definition. It is likely to include public footpaths, bridleways and carriageways. Grass verges are generally regarded as part of the highway. The Regulations make detailed provision for the taking control of goods on a highway. Goods taken control of on a highway may be secured by the use of an immobilisation device. It is for the bailiff to supply the clamp. The bailiff must fix a prominent notice warning of the immobilisation. This notice must be in the prescribed form which is shown at the end of this Chapter. It should place somewhere prominent, such as the windscreen. The bailiff should also supply a notice that the goods have been taken into control. On the Notice the bailiff must provide a twenty-four hour contact telephone number. The clamped vehicle must remain immobilised for a period of at least 2 hours where it is found unless the outstanding sum is paid or an agreement to release it is made. After the period of two hours, the bailiff may remove the vehicle to storage.

If goods being secured on the highway is a motor vehicle, the bailiff may secure them where they are found but he may want to move it to somewhere within a reasonable distance of the location, for example the vehicle might be on double yellow lines or is parked in a dangerous position. If the vehicle is on the highway the bailiff must secure it with an immobilisation device unless the debtor voluntarily hands over the keys. Some internet sites perpetuate the mistake that bailiffs cannot clamp a vehicle and mention the change in law about wheel clamping of vehicles on private property. What is forgotten is that the Protection of Freedoms Act 2012 states at section 54:

54 Offence of immobilising etc. vehicles

(1)A person commits an offence who, without lawful authority—
(a)immobilises a motor vehicle by the attachment to the vehicle, or a part of it, of an immobilising device, or
(b)moves, or restricts the movement of, such a vehicle by any means,

intending to prevent or inhibit the removal of the vehicle by a person otherwise entitled to remove it.

The key words here are, *"**without lawful authority**"*. Bailiffs have lawful authority. The Taking Control of Goods Regulations 2013 specify that an enforcement agent may clamp a vehicle at the *"debtors property"* or on a *'public highway'*. However, a bailiff is not allowed to clamp a vehicle found on any other private land such as supermarket car parks, retail parks, hospital car parks, motorway services or private managed residential car parks.

Removal to a secure place:

There are two types of removal permitted by the TCE Act 2007. These are the removal for the purpose of sale and for taking control of goods. Removal to a secure place is part of the "enforcement stage" where goods are removed as a form of taking control. The goods should only be removed to a secure location that is within a reasonable distance.

Entering into a controlled goods agreement:

The procedure was formerly known as "taking walking possession". A controlled goods agreement is defined as an agreement under which the debtor is permitted to retain possession of the goods but acknowledges that the bailiff has taken control of the goods and the debtor agrees not to remove or dispose of them until the debt is paid. When a bailiff enters into a controlled goods agreement, he or she should consider the person signing the agreement and the authority of the person signing it. A controlled goods agreement may only be made with:

- a debtor aged 16 years or over,
- a person aged over 18 who has been authorised by the debtor to enter into an agreement on his behalf
- a person found to be in "apparent authority" on premises wholly or partly for trade or business purposes. This might be an employee of the business as well as a partner in the business or company officer. However, the Regulations do not define what is apparent authority.
- a person who appears to understand the effect of the agreement and would be capable of entering into it. So a bailiff could not enter into a controlled goods agreement with a mentally disabled person or someone with language difficulties.

The Regulations specify the form of the controlled goods agreement. It must set out:

- the debtor's name and address
- the reference number and date of the agreement
- the bailiff's contact details
- a list of the goods taken into control with sufficient detail of each item to enable the debtor to identify them
- the terms of the arrangement/repayment made with the debtor.

Copies of the agreement should be provided to the signatory and if that person is not the debtor, to the debtor personally. This can be done by leaving a copy of the agreement in a clearly visible place on the premises where goods were taken into control or by delivering it to the premises where goods were taken into control.

The bailiff must provide a notice to the debtor after he has entered premises which gives information about what he is doing. A notice should also be given to the debtor after taking control of goods or entering a vehicle on a highway in order to take control of goods. The notice must be in writing and contain certain things. (The prescribed notice is shown at the end of the previous Chapter.)

The mandatory nature of the new forms of taking control should avoid the practices under the old law which were employed to claim that goods had been levied on. Some of these old practices included cases where the bailiff had not entered the premises and tried to get the debtor to sign a walking possession order at another location. Other examples of bailiffs having claimed levies under the old rules was where a conversation took place on the debtor's doorstep or after looking through the debtor's windows.

Case Example

Bull and Boy HCE Ltd have been instructed by the creditor to enforce a writ of control against Alkward Financing Ltd. The writ is for £10,000 and the enforcement agent attends the offices of Alkward Financing after having the required Notice of intention to take control of goods. The enforcement agent is able to walk into the premises as the doors are not locked. In the offices, there is a large amount of office furniture which the bailiff believes could be taken away and would probably fetch about £7,500 at auction. The enforcement notice states that he intends to take away the items if payment if not received within 7 days. He enters into a controlled goods agreement which is shown at the end of this chapter, and signed by Alison Dawson who is the office receptionist employed through a temping agency. The Controlled Goods Agreement is handed to Alison Dawson and the enforcement officer leaves the premises. When the Managing Director returns from a business meeting, he reads the controlled goods agreement and decides to seek legal advice.

If Alkward Financing seeks legal advice they should be told that there are flaws with the controlled goods agreement. The Regulations are quite clear as to what it must contain. Bull & Boy have not stated on the document what the terms of the arrangement/payment made with the debtor are. There may have been something discussed during the attendance of the HECO but for the controlled goods agreement to be valid it must specify the arrangement. There is also some doubt as to whether or not Alison Dawson had the authority to enter into the controlled goods agreement. For these reasons the controlled goods agreement would not be valid and the HCEO will not have taken control of the goods.

If the bailiff has entered into a controlled goods agreement where the debtor is not a business and it is residential premises and there are flaws in the agreement, when the bailiff returns to remove the goods he will not be able to use force to enter the premises.

What goods of the debtor can a bailiff take ?

Paragraph 3 of Schedule 12 of the TCE Act 2017 defines what is meant by goods of the debtor. There are references in the Schedule to goods of a debtor. It says:

"references to goods of the debtor or another person are references to goods in which the debtor or that person has an interest"

"interest" means a beneficial interest;

The definition as to what are goods of the debtor has recently raised the issue of whether a bailiff can take control of goods on hire purchase. In a case that was heard in the county court in May 2015, the Judge came to the conclusion that a vehicle on hire purchase could be seized by a bailiff. The debtor had issued an injunction after his car had been clamped on the basis that his car was 'supposedly' exempt from being taken given that it was subject to 'Hire Purchase'. The Judge disagreed that the vehicle was 'exempt' stating that the debtor had a 'interest' in the vehicle. The Judgment stated:

"On the drive of the property, it is common ground, was a Saab saloon vehicle, registration number xxxx. This vehicle belonged to Mr S subject to the interest of the finance company — the vehicle having been secured on hire purchase ("HP"). The vehicle against which Mr H was threatening to levy distraint, was therefore the subject of an HP agreement. In fact, Mr H did not have the vehicle recovered — instead, he clamped the Saab vehicle and placed a notice on the window to confirm he had levied on the vehicle.

However, I cannot accept as a matter of law that the fact of an HP agreement per se prohibits a bailiff levying on the vehicle. It will often be the case that the finance company's interest is easily purchased leaving real value to the hirer, who then takes ownership on the discharge of the finance. This is a common matter in relation to excavation equipment, taken out under lease purchase arrangements, where there are agents specialising in arranging finance on such equipment, after the initial finance agreement is bought out. I have tried a number of these cases in the last 12 months in this context.

In principle, I can see no reason to distinguish that type of situation from this.

It is entirely possible, if Mr S had had the lease finance or HP agreement over a period of time, that he would have some real value in the vehicle — there is no reason why the vehicle could have not been levied against, recovered and potentially sold, subject always to the owner, the finance company, having first call on any proceeds.

As I say the likelihood is that the owner would have had its interest bought out before any sale was effected.

(e) As a precaution, and a wise one, Mr H did make a check before he had the Saab removed — having been alerted to the finance issues, he decided not to remove it. However, had he done so, I cannot see any reason in law why it could not lawfully have been done. I cannot find that any ground of complaint can be made out against the actions of Mr H in initially clamping this vehicle, once he had decided to levy against it."

So this Judgment says that it does not automatically mean a vehicle that is subject to finance cannot be taken by a bailiff. A vehicle can be taken in some circumstances if the debtor has a beneficial interest in the vehicle. The matter will depend on the type of finance agreement and the equity (beneficial interest) that may remain in the vehicle.

The bailiff can also take into control goods if they are the sole or joint property of the debtor. Goods which are the sole property of third parties cannot be taken. If goods are seized that are jointly owned by the debtor, that co-owner is entitled to a copy of the inventory, the valuation in preparation of sale and of the notice of the sale that is arranged. If a sale take place, the enforcement agent must first pay the co-owner a share of the proceeds of sale which represents his interest in the goods before dealing with the rest of the proceeds.

Exempt goods

Schedule 12 of the Tribunals, Courts and Enforcement Act 2007 defines exempt goods as:

"goods that regulations exempt by description or circumstances or both"

Regulation 4 of the Taking Control of Goods Regulations 2013 then sets out what goods are "exempt goods" and cannot be taken by a bailiff. This list exempts certain basic and necessary household and business items. The full list contained in Regulation 4 is set out at the end of this Chapter The exemption does not apply where the bailiff is seeking to recover business rates, drainage rates, drainage charges and taxes.

It can be seen from Regulation 4(1)(a), that the exemption for trade items is:

(a) items or equipment (for example, tools, books, telephones, computer equipment and vehicles) which are necessary for use personally by the debtor in the debtor's employment, business, trade, profession, study or education, except that in any case the aggregate value of the items or equipment to which this exemption is applied shall not exceed £1,350;

The key word here is "necessary" and so it important to understand what it means. From looking at past cases, it can be said that "necessary" does not mean:

- Convenient
- Cheaper
- Beneficial to a Business
- Irreplaceable

Example

A High Court Enforcement Officer is instructed to take control of goods at a public house to recover a debt. At the premises, he finds a billiards table and the officer believes it is worth about £2,500 which should be enough to cover the debt of £1,500. The debtor argues with the enforcement officer as he says the billiard table cannot be taken because it was needed for the purposes of trade as a public house.

In this situation, the billiard table would not be an exempt item. It would be regarded as "beneficial" to the business. It would not be regarded as a tool of the trade but merely an addition to the furniture of the pub for the purposes of attracting business.

Regulation 4 (1) (a) also provides an aggregate value for exempt items of £1,350. This is to prevent businesses from claiming all equipment as necessary trade items. So a business when faced with a bailiff will have to decide a number of limited important items of trade equipment

72

that fall within the £1,350 limit. Regulation 5 includes the further exemption of preventing the seizure of the debtor's only or principal home. This creates protection against the seizure of tents, caravans and mobile homes which did not previously exist.

Can a Bailiff take cash ?

It is now debatable whether a bailiff can seize cash. The statutory powers permitting this have been repealed and there is no mention of the right in the new Act and Regulations. The Regulations refer to the taking of "goods" but money is not regarded as "goods". However, it is possible that "cash" is covered by the provisions that permit a bailiff to take promissory notes and a bank note is a form of promissory note.

What if the debtors claims that a bailiff has taken control of exempt goods?

If a debtor believes the goods taken into control are "exempt goods" then he must within 7 days of the removal give notice in writing to the enforcement agent of the claim and the notice must include:

(a) their full name and address and that address is their address for service;
(b) a list of all those goods in respect of which they make such a claim; and
(c) the grounds of the claim in respect of each item.

On receipt of the notice, the enforcement agent must within 3 days give a copy of the notice to the creditor. The creditor must respond within 7 days saying whether the claim to exempt goods is admitted or disputed in whole or in part. If the creditor admits the exempt goods claim, the creditor is not liable for any fees and expenses incurred after receipt of the notice. If a creditor fails to give the required notice within 7 days, the enforcement agent can apply to the court for directions.

If the creditor disputes the claim for exempt goods, then the debtor if he wants to pursue the matter must make an application to the court within 7 days. There is one important difference between the application in respect of exempt goods and third party claims to goods, which is that when claiming the goods are exempt no payment into court to cover the value of the goods is required. However, making an application in respect of alleged exempt goods does not place a stay (a stop) on the sale of the goods. Therefore, the application should request a stay on sale of the goods pending a court hearing to decide the issue.

Taking control of goods belonging to a spouse

It is not uncommon for bailiffs to try and take control of goods belonging to one spouse to settle the debts of the other. If goods are bought with joint money then it might be that the goods are jointly owned. If one spouse purchases chattels from the other there is no reason not to treat it as a valid transfer that would defeat a creditor seeking to execute a judgment. A potential issue arises in respect of items bought by a couple after marriage (or after they begin to live together). The courts generally assume an intention to share property acquired and so may allocate beneficial interests in it equally.

74

Insolvency and bailiff action

If a creditor obtains a money judgment against a debtor, whether the debtor will pay will obviously depend to a large degree on the circumstances of the judgment debtor. If a debtor has not paid the creditor because he or the business is in financial difficulties then the issues of insolvency or bankruptcy of the judgment debtor may arise at the time the bailiff is seeking to take control of goods. The presentation of a petition for the winding up of a company or for the bankruptcy of an individual will impact on the actions of the bailiff.

The general principle is that where the execution has been completed prior to the commencement of insolvency proceedings (the date of the presentation of the petition in a liquidation or the date of the order in a bankruptcy), the creditor will be entitled to retain the benefit of the execution. The important question is at what point will it be deemed that the bailiff has completed the execution of a warrant? The legislation provides that the taking control of goods process is completed by seizure and sale, or by the making of a charging order. However, it has been held that the process is not complete if monies are still in the hands of the enforcement agent. Therefore, if the enforcement agent charged with the execution still holds the proceeds of sale or goods on receipt of the notice of the insolvency, he/she must pass the funds or goods to the liquidator or trustee. If the judgment debt is greater than £500 in relation to a company or £1,000 in relation to an individual, the enforcement agent must hold the proceeds from the sale of controlled goods or monies paid to avoid a sale, for a period of 14 days pending the presentation of any petition for winding-up or bankruptcy. If the enforcement agent receives notice of an insolvency petition within the 14 days in which they are required to hold the proceeds, he/she must hold any funds for the liquidator or trustee if an order is subsequently made.

Consider the following examples:

1. The Judgment creditor has obtained a writ of control in respect of a a Judgment debt of £10,000 against a the Judgment Debtor that is a limited company. The High Court Enforcement officer attends the premises and takes control of a vehicle owned by the debtor valued at £20,000. The HCEO enters into a controlled goods agreement but then a few days later, the HCEO received notice that a winding up petition had been presented by another creditor of the Judgment debtor. Should the goods that are the subject of a controlled goods agreement be given to the liquidator?

2. The Judgment Creditor instructs an HCEO to take control of goods belonging to an individual debtor. The bailiff recovers £6000 from the debtor by way of a cash payment on the 1st January. On the 10 January, the HCEO receives notice that a bankruptcy order is made against the judgment debtor. Does the £6,000 have to be given to the trustee in bankruptcy?

In example 1 above, the execution process by the bailiff has not been completed because although the goods have been seized under a controlled goods agreement, there has not been a sale and so the goods that form part of the controlled goods agreement should be passed to the liquidator as part of the insolvent's estate and for the benefit of all creditors. In example 2, the £6,000 should also be passed to the trustee in bankruptcy because again the execution process had not completed because a bankruptcy order had been made within 14 days of the bailiff receiving the monies paid to avoid a sale.

There are some occasions where a creditor faced with a situation illustrated by the above examples could apply to the court to set aside the rights of the liquidator but this discretion is exercised in limited cases and usually where there has been impropriety on the part of the debtor before or after judgment. So the question is, what types of situations are those that a court might set aside the rights of the liquidator? These situations are regarded as rare but might include where there has been a deception of the bailiffs or use of the winding-up procedure as a deliberate way of avoiding payment.

Case example:

Southern Coast Consultancies have been pursuing fees due from Ross Care Homes for services they have provided to help them get through a local authority Inspection. After obtaining a Judgment, Southern Coast instruct an HCEO to recover the debt due to them. The HECO sends the Notice of Intention to attend and take control of goods. When they attend the premises, they are met by a person who says that they have never heard of Ross Care Homes at that address and produces what purports to be a lease between another company and the landlord of the premises. The HCEO refers back to

Southern Coast for instructions. This takes a few days. Southern Coast obtain information from a person who is working for Ross Care Homes which indicates that they are still operating from those premises. The bailiff returns on the instructions of Southern Coast and on this next occasion another person appears who claims that he is the landlord and that he owns all the items within the property. He waves documents which allegedly show him as being the landlord. The HCEO returns to the office to check who the owner of the premises is and a search of the land registry confirms that the person who claimed to be the landlord is not the owner of the premises. The bailiff makes a further visit to the premises and enters into a controlled goods agreement. Seven days after the bailiff enters into the controlled goods agreement, a Notice of Meeting of Creditors is received from an Insolvency Practitioner.

****

Application notice

For help in completing this form please read the notes for guidance form N244Notes.

In the	Upton District Registry of the High Court

Claim no.	UP123WQ12
Fee Account no.	
Warrant no. (if applicable)	AP100098
Claimant's name (including ref.)	Phones and Gadgets R US Ltd
Defendant's name (including ref.)	Brian Parker
Date	

1. What is your name or, if you are a legal representative, the name of your firm?

2. Are you a
   - [ ] Claimant
   - [✓] Defendant
   - [ ] Legal Representative
   - [ ] Other *(please specify)*

   If you are a legal representative whom do you represent?

3. What order are you asking the court to make and why?

   I am seeking an order that goods taken by Carefree Bailiffs are returned to me and damages paid because the Enforcement Agent was in breach of Regulation 10 of the Taking Control of Goods Regulations 2013 because the only person on the premises was a vulnerable person.

4. Have you attached a draft of the order you are applying for? [✓] Yes [ ] No

5. How do you want to have this application dealt with? [✓] at a hearing [ ] without a hearing [ ] at a telephone hearing

6. How long do you think the hearing will last? [ ] Hours 30 Minutes

   Is this time estimate agreed by all parties? [ ] Yes [✓] No

7. Give details of any fixed trial date or period

   None

8. What level of Judge does your hearing need?

   District Judge

9. Who should be served with this application?

   Claimant and Carefree Bailiffs Ltd

9a. Please give the service address, (other than details of the claimant or defendant) of any party named in question 9.

   Carefree Bailifs Ltd
   10 Market Road,
   Upton

Controlled goods agreement

Name of Debtor

Alkward Financing Ltd

Address

10 Manor Road
Upmarket
UP10 2 PN

Enforcement agent reference number(s)

999/123/XXX

About this agreement

By entering this agreement the debtor will be able to continue to use the goods listed in this agreement. The debtor acknowledges that these goods are under the control of the enforcement agent until the sum outstanding is paid in full. The debtor agrees that they will not remove or dispose of these goods, or allow anyone else to, during this time.

If the debtor does not stick to the terms of this agreement the debtor's goods may be removed, or secured on site (commercial premises only) and sold. This will incur a further fee.

Enforcement details

Details of the court judgment or order or enforcement power by virtue of which the debt is enforceable

Judgment in favour of A Smith Ltd entered in Upmarket County Court in Case No. BX000123RT on xx/xx/xx
Writ of Control issued on the _____ for the sum of £_____

Sum outstanding

Debt	£10,000
Interest	£250.00
Compliance stage fee	£90.00
Enforcement stage fee	£228.00
Expenses (if any)	
TOTAL sum outstanding	£10568.00

Please detail the expenses

(as at the date of this notice)

Arrangement terms

The terms of this controlled goods agreement are set out below.

Signature

A Dawson   (Temporary Receptionist)   **Date** | 1 | 2 | / | 0 | 2 | / | 2 | 0 | 1 | 5 |

Debtor, person authorised by the debtor or person in apparent authority

Print name

ALISON DAWSON

Signature

A Bull   **Date** | 1 | 2 | / | 0 | 2 | / | 2 | 0 | 1 | 5 |

Enforcement Agent

Print name

ANDREW BULL

How you can contact the enforcement agent or the enforcement agent's office

Telephone

| 01234 1112345 |

Address

| Bull & Boy HCE Ltd
123 Hampton Road
Upmarket
UP2 4NM |

Opening hours and days

| 8am to 7pm Monday to Saturday |

You can seek free advice and information from

AdviceUK at www.adviceuk.org.uk/find-a-member

National Debtline at www.nationaldebtline.org or on 0808 808 4000

Money Advice Service at www.moneyadviceservice.org.uk or on 0300 500 5000

Gov.uk at www.gov.uk

Other free advice is available.

Goods taken into control

Description of item (eg. Computer, television, car etc.)	Manufacturer (if known)	Model (if known)	Serial number (if known) or Registration mark if a vehicle	Material, colour and usage of the goods or any other identifying characteristics
Computer	Acer		COM12345678	
Computer	HP		TV23456789	
Computer	Dell		FR12345679	
Computer	Dell		NY23456789	
Computer	HP		VG1234356	
Office Furniture				
Printer	HP		BY123456789	
Printer	HP		BNQe1234567	
Telephone System	LG		123LG123	

82

Warning
of immobilisation

Please read this warning - it is important

This is to tell you that I have fitted a device to secure your vehicle(s)/goods and prevent them from being moved.

Date and time vehicles(s)/ goods were secured

Date [ ] / [ ] / [   ]

Time [   ]

I have done this because you have not paid the sum outstanding.

Further information

To discuss this matter please telephone

[   ]

quoting reference or reference numbers

[   ]

Signature

_____

Enforcement Agent

_____

PRINT NAME

You can seek free advice and information from

AdviceUK at www.adviceuk.org.uk/find-a-member

National Debtline at www.nationaldebtline.org or on 0808 808 4000

Money Advice Service at www.moneyadviceservice.org.uk or on 0300 500 5000

Gov.uk at www.gov.uk

Other free advice is available.

The Taking Control of Goods Regulations 2013

PART 1

INTRODUCTORY

Exempt Goods

Exempt goods

4.—(1) Subject to paragraph (2) and to regulation 5, the following goods of the debtor are exempt goods—

(a) items or equipment (for example, tools, books, telephones, computer equipment and vehicles) which are necessary for use personally by the debtor in the debtor's employment, business, trade, profession, study or education, except that in any case the aggregate value of the items or equipment to which this exemption is applied shall not exceed £1,350;

(b) such clothing, bedding, furniture, household equipment, items and provisions as are reasonably required to satisfy the basic domestic needs of the debtor and every member of the debtor's household, including (but not restricted to)—

(i) a cooker or microwave;

(ii) a refrigerator;

(iii) a washing machine;

(iv) a dining table large enough, and sufficient dining chairs, to seat the debtor and every member of the debtor's household;

(v) beds and bedding sufficient for the debtor and every member of the debtor's household;

(vi) one landline telephone, or if there is no landline telephone at the premises, a mobile or internet telephone which may be used by the debtor or a member of the debtor's household;

(vii) any item or equipment reasonably required for—

(aa) the medical care of the debtor or any member of the debtor's household;

(bb) safety in the dwelling-house; or

(cc) the security of the dwelling-house (for example, an alarm system) or security in the dwelling-house;

(viii) sufficient lamps or stoves, or other appliance designed to provide lighting or heating facilities, to satisfy the basic heating and lighting needs of the debtor's household; and

(ix) any item or equipment reasonably required for the care of—

(aa) a person under the age of 18;

(bb) a disabled person; or

(cc) an older person;

(c) assistance dogs (including guide dogs, hearing dogs and dogs for disabled persons), sheep dogs, guard dogs or domestic pets;

(d) a vehicle on which a valid disabled person's badge is displayed because it is used for, or in relation to which there are reasonable grounds for believing that it is used for, the carriage of a disabled person;

(e) a vehicle (whether in public ownership or not) which is being used for, or in relation to which there are reasonable grounds for believing that it is used for, police, fire or ambulance purposes; and

(f) a vehicle displaying a valid British Medical Association badge or other health emergency badge because it is being used for, or in relation to which there are reasonable grounds for believing that it is used for, health emergency purposes.

(2) Paragraph (1)(a) does not apply where the debt is being enforced under—

(i) section 62A of the Local Government Finance Act 1988(**1**);

(ii) section 54 of the Land Drainage Act 1991(**2**);

(iii) paragraph 12 of Schedule 15 to the Water Resources Act 1991(**3**); or

(iv) section 127 of the Finance Act 2008(**4**).

Part 6

Third Party Goods

Other than jointly owned and partnership property, goods owned wholly by a third party cannot be taken into control. The Taking Control of Goods National Standards 2014 advises bailiffs not to take control or remove goods that clearly belong to a third party who is not responsible for the debt. Where a claim of ownership is made, the third party should be given clear information on the process to follow to recover the goods. The bailiff should use common sense and plausible claims to goods should be considered. Although it is not the responsibility of the Bailiff to determine ownership, he has a duty not to waste the courts time and incur unnecessary litigation expense for the creditor. The bailiff may be called upon to justify to a Judge why he had reasonable grounds to believe that the goods taken control of were that of the debtor. So the bailiff should not knowingly take control of goods when he had been shown valid proof of ownership.

If the third party's claim cannot be resolved by negotiation, then ultimately that third party should follow the procedure laid down for resolving such matters. The procedure is contained in Schedule 12 , Part 2, Paragraph 60 of the TCE Act. Once this claim is received the Enforcement Agent should direct the third party making the claim to make the claim in writing to the creditor via the Enforcement Agent. The claim should contain the claimant's full name and address, list of all goods claimed and grounds for claim for each item.

When Enforcement Agents receive third party claims, they should, within 3 days of getting the claim, send it to the creditor for them to admit or dispute. The creditor has a further 7 days to respond to the Enforcement Agent as to whether or not they dispute or admit the claim. If they admit the claim the Enforcement Agent should withdraw from the control of the goods and allow the third party to collect them. If the creditor disputes the claim the Enforcement Agent should write to the third party within 3 days of receipt from the creditor of the answer. It is then up to the third party to issue an application to the county court against the creditor. The third party may be required to pay into the court an amount equal to the value of the goods or a proportion as directed by the court or the Enforcement Agents costs of keeping the goods.

Fred Smith v Jeff Appleyard

Fred Smith had been having financial problems. Jeff Appleyard agrees to lend Fred the sum of £15,000 to help him through his difficulties. Rather carelessly, Jeff does not get his loan secured on Fred's property. Jeff says that Fred can pay him back in 12 months. Fred fails to repay the loan and Jeff issues a claim and obtains a County Court Judgment. Fred assures Jeff that he will settle the Judgment debt as he has a boat worth £20,000 which he is going to sell to clear the loan. Jeff has not seen Fred's boat but agrees to give him a little more time to sell it and come up with the money. However, after being very patient, Jeff still does not receive payment and decides to instruct a High Court Enforcement Officer to enforce the Judgment. The Enforcement agent arrives at the home of Fred on 1 July 2015. The property has a long and wide driveway up to the house. On the drive is a canal boat in very good condition. The enforcement agent telephones a colleague and takes advice as to how much the boat could be worth. It is suggested to him that it could be worth around £20,000. The Enforcement Agent secures the boat on the drive. Fred tells the enforcement agent that it is not his boat and that it belongs to his friend Michael. If Michael wants to claim the boat is his he must put in a "third party claim". How does Michael claim ownership of the boat?

In the example above, Michael must first send a letter to the Enforcement Agent within 7 days of the goods having been taken, giving details of his name and address (and stating the address where documents can be served), a list of the items claimed and state the ground of the claim for each item.

Dear Sirs

Re: Jeff Appleyard v. Fred Smith
Court claim Number: AB04YU12
Your ref: HC1234

I write to claim ownership of the goods which you have taken control of at 40 Bighouse Manor, Newtown, NW10 3ER.

My name: Michael Cane
Address: 123 Littlehouse, Newtown, NT12 3DS

The goods which you have taken control of which I claim ownership of are:

Canal boat named "Autumn Days"

This boat was parked on the drive of Fred Smith because I did not have room to park it on my property. I purchased this boat from John Seafare in 2010.

Yours faithfully

Michael Cane

Upon receipt of this letter from Michael Cane, the Enforcement Agent should send it to the creditor within 3 days. On receipt of the third party claim, Jeff considers the merits of it. Jeff is suspicious of the fact that Michael has no documentary evidence to support the fact that he owns the boat. If the boat was used or kept on UK inland waters or canals, then it must be registered or licenced. So one would have expected the canal boat to be registered. He tells the Enforcement Agent that he rejects the third party claim by Michael Cane. If Mr Cane wants to pursue the claim of ownership to the boat, then he must make an application to the court. The procedure for making such an application is contained in Part 85 of the Civil procedure Rules ("CPR"). The application must be made to the court that issued the warrant or if the warrant was issued under an Act, to the debtor's home court.

There have been reports of people seeking injunctions in situations where they are attempting to stop a bailiff taking control of goods where it is claimed a third party owns the goods. Seeking an injunction stopping the bailiff is not the correct procedure and district judges have been reminding these litigants in person that the correct procedure to follow is in CPR Part 85. The controversial part of the new process for a third party claiming ownership of goods taken by a bailiff is the requirement to pay a proportion of the value of the goods when making the application.

The required payments under paragraph 60 of Schedule 12 in the TCE 2007 is an amount *"equal to the value of the goods, or to a proportion of it directed by the court"*. This could cause injustice to a third party with a genuine claim to the goods in situations where the creditor has taken a hard line and disputes the third party's claim to the goods. This is a change from the old procedure whereby if the claim to the goods was disputed, the bailiff would refer the matter to the court for an "inter-pleader" hearing at which a judge would decide ownership. Now, it is for the third party claiming title to the goods to make the application and consequently they will have to pay a court fee to make the application and a proportion of the value of the goods. It is arguable that such a change was needed to avoid claims without merit, but it is quite easy to see that this new procedure could lead to injustice. When the party makes an application, it is permitted to seek further directions at court for leave to pay only a proportion of the value of the goods.

The Application which a third party has to make to claim back goods they allege belong to them is made on form N244. A completed example is shown at the end of this Chapter. This court application by Mr Cane exhibits a letter from Mr Seafare as well as an application to the Environment Agency.

The weak aspects of Michael Cane's third party claim is the lack of documentation. The paper work he has produced is not contemporaneous and is after the event. A cynic might say that the letter from Mr Seafare and the application to the Environment Agency, both dated after the bailiff took control of the boat, have been concocted to make it look as though Michael Cane owns the boat. On the other hand, it is entirely possible that Michael Cane does not have any actual purchase document from 5 years ago and that he has not until recently wanted to use the boat on inland waterways, thus his application for a licence. Also, you might wonder why he would be prepared to pay a court fee and a proportion of the boats value if he did not own it. He has signed a statement of truth on the N244 application form and he is at risk of contempt of court if he knowingly gives false information. As to the request to only pay a proportion of the boats value, although it is early days in regards to the new procedure, there are indications that District Judges will permit the third party claimant to pay a low proportion of the value of the item claimed.

****

Application notice

For help in completing this form please read the
notes for guidance form N244Notes.

In the	Newton District Registry of the High Court
Claim no.	AX100445NN
Fee Account no.	
Warrant no. (if applicable)	123WARR
Claimant's name (including ref.)	Jeff Appleyard
Defendant's name (including ref.)	Fred Smith
Date	xx/xx/xx

1. What is your name or, if you are a legal representative, the name of your firm?

2. Are you a   ☐ Claimant   ☐ Defendant   ☐ Legal Representative

   ☑ Other *(please specify)*   Third Party claiming owership to controlled goods

   If you are a legal representative whom do you represent?

3. What order are you asking the court to make and why?

   I, Michael Cane, of 10 Gold Street, Newton, wish to make a claim against the controlled goods taken
   under this warrant. I seek an Order that the goods are returned to me. I also ask the court to direct
   that I do not have to pay an amount equal to the value of the goods or that I pay a smaller proportion.

4. Have you attached a draft of the order you are applying for?   ☑ Yes   ☐ No

5. How do you want to have this application dealt with?   ☑ at a hearing   ☐ without a hearing

   ☐ at a telephone hearing

6. How long do you think the hearing will last?   ☐ Hours   30 Minutes

   Is this time estimate agreed by all parties?   ☐ Yes   ☑ No

7. Give details of any fixed trial date or period   None

8. What level of Judge does your hearing need?   District Judge

9. Who should be served with this application?   Jeff Appleyard & Enforcement Agent

9a. Please give the service address, (other than details of the
    claimant or defendant) of any party named in question 9.

92

10. What information will you be relying on, in support of your application?

☐ the attached witness statement

☐ the statement of case

☑ the evidence set out in the box below

If necessary, please continue on a separate sheet.
1. The boat that was seized by the Enforcement Agent from the drive of Fred Smith on 15 Nov 2015 belongs to me. I purchased the sailing boat from John Seafare in 2010. I paid Mr Seafare £25,000 for it but unfortunately I do not have the bill of sale. I have however obtained a letter from Mr Seafare confirming that I did in fact purchase the boat from him. This letter is attached and marked "Exhibit 1".

2. I am intending to use the sailing boat on the River Thames and therefore I have applied for the required licence. I attach a copy of my application to the Environment Agency dated the 7 July 2015 for a licence to use the boat on the Thames. This is attached and marked "Exhibit 2".

3. The boat is worth about £20,000. I am aware that on making this application there is a requirement to pay a deposit equal to the value of the goods to which ownership is being claimed. I ask the court to direct that I do not have to pay a sum equal to the whole value of the goods as I simply cannot afford that and it would be unjust. If the court orders me to pay a sum on making this application, then I ask that it be a smaller and reasonable sum. I attach details of my income and outgoings. I could only afford to pay £500.

Statement of Truth

(I believe) (The applicant believes) that the facts stated in this section (and any continuation sheets) are true.

Signed _____ Dated _____

Applicant('s legal representative)('s litigation friend)

Full name MICHAEL CANE

Name of applicant's legal representative's firm _____

Position or office held _____
(if signing on behalf of firm or company)

11. Signature and address details

Signed _____ Dated 20 December 2015

Applicant('s legal representative's)('s litigation friend)

Position or office held _____
(if signing on behalf of firm or company)

Applicant's address to which documents about this application should be sent

10 Gold Street Newton	If applicable	
	Phone no.	0900 999666
	Fax no.	
	DX no.	
Postcode N N 1 7 H K	Ref no.	

E-mail address	

Part 7

Remedies for Debtors and Creditors

If a debtor believes the bailiff has breached the procedure for taking control of goods, Schedule 12 of the TCE Act 2007 provides debtors with a remedy. An aggrieved debtor may bring proceedings under paragraph 66 of Schedule 12 for redress for any wrongful or irregular act by an enforcement agent. The court could order goods to be returned to the debtor as well as ordering the enforcement agent or related party (which could be the person on whom the enforcement power is conferred or the creditor) to pay damages in respect of any loss suffered by the debtor as a direct result of the breach or anything done under the defective enforcement document. The power of the court to award damages does not apply where the enforcement agent acted in the reasonable belief that he was not breaching a provision of Schedule 12 or that the instrument (document of enforcement) was defective.

In the example of **Carefree Bailiffs v Brian Parker,** which was discussed in an earlier Chapter, Mr Parker was able to take action against the bailiff under Schedule 12 because at the time of taking control of the goods, the only person on the premises was a vulnerable person. He was able to claim the return of goods and seek damages.

A cursory search of the internet reveals that local authorities have increased the use of bailiffs by a significant amount. It is not just Councils in areas that might be perceived as having social problems that there has been a big increase in use; the increase is in all parts of the country. Figures for the financial year of 2014/15 show that bailiffs made 2.1 million visits on the instruction of Councils. Council leaders insist that the use of bailiffs is regarded as the last resort, but reiterate the fact that they have a responsibility to all tax payers to chase debts.

With more bailiff visits and an increased focus on bailiff behaviour in light of the recent reforms and prime time television programmes, one might not be surprised if there are more complaints about the conduct of bailiffs. It does not mean that because people are complaining more about something that the bailiffs are necessarily doing anything wrong. In these more informed times with all sorts of information available on the internet and elsewhere, people have a greater awareness of how to make a complaint if a bailiff does not conform to the standards expected.

The new Taking Control of Goods Regulations 2013 was introduced on 6th April 2014 and this has significantly changed the way in which debts can be enforced by a bailiff/enforcement agent. The changes include the introduction of 'fixed fees' and additional improvements have also been made to 'exempt goods'. A further improvement is the requirement for a bailiff/enforcement agent to provide statutory notices to the debtor. By far the greatest improvement has been the introduction of a 'Compliance stage' allowing a debtor the opportunity to avoid a bailiff visit (and fees of £235) by outlining a sensible payment proposal. These amendments will substantially reduce the number of complaints being made. However, if you are seeking to make a complaint about any aspect of bailiff enforcement then the following outlines what you can do.

If you are wanting to complain about the conduct of a bailiff instructed by a local authority then you could complain to the local authority and then ultimately The Local Government Ombudsman.

Complaining to a Local Authority

When a bailiff is instructed by a local authority, he is acting as the agent of the Council. So any letter of complaint to the bailiff company should be copied to the local authority. As the bailiff is acting as the agent of the local authority, the council is responsible for the acts and omissions of their agents.

How to complain about a bailiff acting for a local authority

Many local authorities will attempt to say that all complaints should be directed to the bailiff company. However, the bailiff is acting as the agent for the local authority and so the council is responsible for the acts and omissions of their agents.

The first stage of a complaint about a bailiff acting for a local authority is to write a letter to the chief executive making it clear that it is a formal complaint. It is unlikely that the letter will actually be read by the chief executive but marking it in this way will make it clear that you wish to register a formal complaint. You will most likely receive contact from a senior member of staff whose job it is to respond to complaints. They will probably send out a copy of their complaints procedure.

When writing a formal complaint it is important to try and write a structured letter that sets out the facts as you see them and explain concisely why you are unhappy with the conduct of the bailiff. A good letter of complaint will avoid being a long and rambling rant about everything you dislike about bailiffs. Stick to the facts and avoid sarcasm; state the outcome you are seeking.

Once you have been through the complete complaints process of the local authority, if you are not satisfied with the response then you might want to consider taking your complaint to the local government ombudsman. An Ombudsman will probably not consider a complaint until you have received the final response from the council. The local government ombudsman can consider concerns regarding the actions of a bailiff/ enforcement officer collecting council tax, NNDR (Non-Domestic Rates, or Business Rates) and road traffic debts such as parking fines. An ombudsman may refuse to consider a complaint where an independent right of appeal already exists, for example with a parking charge notice a right of appeal against it exists. The ombudsman is usually only concerned with service levels and whether the actions of those complained about were fair and reasonable. Under its powers the local government ombudsman investigates complaints about maladministration and service failure. If there has been either of these faults then it can consider a remedy if the fault has caused an adverse impact or has caused the complainant injustice. The ombudsman is not going to consider the legalities of every situation. So if for example you have a complaint that a bailiff has taken a vehicle that belongs to a third party, the method of resolving such a dispute would be for that third party to bring a third party claim in the way explained earlier in this book.

Since April 2013, the local government ombudsman publishes on its website decisions of all complaints received. There are different categories of decision:

- Upheld - this is where the local government ombudsman finds fault with the local authority.

- Not upheld - this is where the local government ombudsman did not find the local authority at fault.

- Closed after initial enquiries - this is where the matter may not be in the ombudsman's jurisdiction such as there being a right of appeal or there is not enough evidence of fault to investigate.

The local government ombudsman's website contains a searchable database of decisions and is a useful source of information as to the types of cases they investigate and the type of remedy they might impose if a complaint is upheld. An example of a complaint that concerned the actions of the councils bailiff when visiting a shop to recover outstanding costs for a business rate debt involved **Lancaster City Council and Mrs B**. The decisions do not name the complainant hence the reference to Mrs B. The decision was delivered on 23 July 2015.

Mrs B owned a shop. The council sent her a bill for non-domestic rates in March 2013. By January 2014, a bill was due for payment and at that date she still owed £1020 of the original bill which was £5204.70. At the end of January, the magistrates court issued a liability order for £610. In March, Mrs B paid the council £610. The payment covered her last instalment and the councils court costs but did not cover the bailiffs fees. A bailiff visited the shop in September 2014 to collect in full the payment due or remove goods. The bailiff wore a body camera and could be heard in a loud voice asking everyone to leave the shop as well as saying he was there to enforce payment of bailiffs costs. Mrs B complained that the bailiff was out of order during the visit. She says it was all very embarrassing and bad for business.

Findings in Mrs B v. Lancaster City Council

The ombudsman upheld Mrs B's complaint in that the bailiff's conduct was not in accordance with the civil enforcement associations code of practice or the council's and bailiffs contract and its own code of practice. The ombudsman found that there was:

– No reason why the bailiff should have asked everyone to leave the shop and by doing so was bound to cause embarrassment to Mrs B.

- The bailiff should not have said remove everything of value in the shop. That was not proportional to the value of the costs and misrepresented the bailiffs powers.

- The bailiff was not justified in adding a £70 waiting fee or saying he would charge £70 for each hour he was there. The contract with the council was that the bailiff was allowed to charge a £70 per hour waiting fee only after an hour had already elapsed.

The bailiff company agreed to refund the £70 fee. The agreed action held an appropriate remedy for the injustice caused to Mrs B by the bailiff's fault.

In another decision by the local government ombudsman, a complaint by **Mr B against Reading Borough Council** was not upheld. (The complete decision can be viewed on the local government ombudsman website.) In this decision, the ombudsman considered a complaint about bailiff fees added to two bus lane contravention penalty charges incurred during 2014. The complainant incurred two penalty charges for the bus lane contraventions. He did not dispute the penalties. The council sent the penalty charge notices and all subsequent correspondence to the registered address for Mr B's vehicle. He left the property and let it to a tenant. However, he failed to notify the DVLA of his change of address. He returned to the property on 27 July 2014 to collect his post. By this time the council had obtained orders from the Traffic Enforcement Centre to recover the penalty charges. The orders required Mr B to either pay the charge or make a statutory declaration in writing. He did neither. He telephoned the Council on 28 July 2014. In fact he made five telephone calls to the council. He did not however pay the charges. He says that he spoke to a person who told him to write to the council and was promised the council would look again at the charges. His letter arrived on 4 August 2014 a week after his telephone calls.

The council issued a warrant to the bailiffs to collect the unpaid penalties on 31 July 2014. The bailiffs sent letters to the property which Mr B was letting out. The bailiffs received no response so an enforcement agent visited the property on 2 September 2014 where they met the tenant. The tenant contacted Mr B and he paid the bailiffs straight away. As a result of the visit he incurred enforcement fees of £235 as well as compliance fees of £75 in addition to the £97 penalty charges. Mr B complained that he did not believe he should have to pay the bailiffs fees because he says the council was at fault for issuing a warrant after telling him on the telephone to write to the council and for failing to pass on his new address to the bailiffs on receipt of his letter of 4 August. He complained to the council who investigated and decided that they had followed the correct procedures. It said it was unable to investigate the complaint about the telephone call on 28 July because it had no record of the call.

Findings in Mr B v. Reading Borough Council

Mr B acknowledged that he was largely the author of his own misfortune. However, he complained that the fault of the Council frustrated his efforts to mitigate the impact of his own errors. The case turned on the telephone call he made to the Council on 28 July 2014

101

and the advice he says he was given during that call. The Ombudsman said that the problem was that they had no way of knowing what was said. The Ombudsman discontinued the investigation as there was not enough evidence to reach a decision.

The decisions of the Local Government Ombudsman can be viewed at the following website page: www.lgo.org.uk/decisions/search

Complaining about a Certificated Bailiff to the County Court

A complaint to the County Court about a bailiff should always be a last resort and in particular, when the new bailiff regulations came into effect on 6th April 2014 significant changes were imposed regarding such complaints. Up until 6th April 2014 complaints to the court regarding the conduct of a bailiff were made by way of a simple form called a 'Form 4' . There is no longer such a form and the form for a complaint is merely referred to as an 'Enforcement Agent Complaint'.

Under Regulation 9(1) of The Certification of Enforcement Agents Regulations 2014, any person who considers that a certificated person is by reason of the certificated person's conduct in acting as an enforcement agent, or for any other reason, not a fit person to hold a certificate, may submit a complaint in writing to the court.

The procedure for submitting complaints about the fitness of a bailiff to hold a certificate are contained in the Civil Procedure Rules 84.20(4).

102

Complaints as to fitness to hold a certificate
84.20

(1) This rule applies to a complaint under regulation 9(1) of the Certification Regulations.

(2) The complaint must be submitted to the County Court hearing centre at which the certificate was issued, using the relevant form prescribed in Practice Direction 4.

(3) A copy of the complaint must be sent to the applicant at least 14 days before the hearing, and the applicant may respond both in writing and at the hearing.

(4) The complainant is not liable for any costs incurred by the certificated person in responding to the complaint, unless paragraph (5) applies.

(5) The court may order the complainant to pay such costs as it considers reasonable if it is satisfied that the complaint—

(a) discloses no reasonable grounds for considering that the certificated person is not a fit person to hold a certificate; and

(b) amounts to an abuse of the court's process.

Before the new rules were introduced there was a significant number of complaints made on "Form 4". Many of these "Form 4" were encouraged by self proclaimed experts on the internet as a method of causing trouble for bailiffs who they claimed had not followed the correct procedure. A large number of these complaints were regarded as having no foundation and were regarded as an abuse of the court process. For this reason, CPR Part 84.20(5) contains provision for costs to be awarded against the complainant if the complaint does not show reasonable grounds for considering a person is not fit to hold a certificate.

An example of a case where a complaint about a certificated bailiff led to the bailiff having his licence revoked for 6 months was heard in March 2014. Although the case happened before the new regulations came into effect, the circumstances in that case give an indication of the type of conduct which could lead to a bailiff's certificate being revoked.

The incident which led to the Judge revoking the bailiff's certificate happened when the bailiff was trying to collect an unpaid TV licence debt of £78 dating back to 2002 on August 22, 2013. The court heard that when he knocked on the door, a 12-year-old came to an upstairs window. The bailiff demanded that the 12 year old come downstairs and gave her a note to pass onto her mother, on which he had written that if the debt was not paid by the end of that day, he would return with police '*tonight*' and her mother would be arrested. He wrote on the note: "*Police will enter your property to arrest you and detain you in custody. Final warning, I will return with police tonight.*" The bailiff claimed the girl answered the door when he knocked on it, and that there was no incident involving an upstairs window. Another note was left on September 4 when the bailiff attended the property with two police officers.

The court heard the first letter was not sealed in a proper envelope, as it should have been, and that the alterations to the notice and the repeated use of the word "Police" had been made with an intention to cause alarm. The fact this letter was handed to a 12-year-old girl was an aggravating feature, a judge ruled. The judge also said that his certificate would likely have been revoked even if this note had been handed to an adult.

Complaining about a High Court Enforcement Officer

The High Court Enforcement Officers Association can consider complaints about High Court Enforcement Officers in respect of the way they enforced High Court Writs of Control or Writs of Possession. The way to complain is set out on their website: www.hceoa.org.uk

Complaining about a Private Certificated Bailiff to the Civil Enforcement Association

The Civil Enforcement Association is an independently funded association formed to represent all private certificated bailiffs in England and Wales. Details of their complaints procedure can be obtained from their website: www.civea.co.uk

New offence of obstructing an enforcement officer

Under schedule 12 paragraph 68 a person is guilty of an offence if he intentionally obstructs a person lawfully acting as an enforcement agent. There is also an offence of intentionally interfering with control goods without lawful excuse. A person found guilty of these offences may be liable to a fine or imprisonment not exceeding 51 weeks. The new offence refers to a person acting 'intentionally', this means that the individual must act with the deliberate intention of making life difficult for the bailiff. It is not necessary to display hostility nor is the motive relevant. The key point is whether he intended to inhibit the bailiff in his duties. Not only may the debtor be guilty of the offence of obstructing an enforcement agent but he might also be in criminal contempt. The use of violence and threats of violence to eject a bailiff from premises could also lead to a prosecution for assault or an action for trespass to the person.

Case example

Downton Housing Association and Mr Garry Brownlow

Downton housing association has obtained a possession order against Mr Gary Brownlow. The county court bailiff and Miss Fiona Proctor from the housing association, attend on the date for the eviction. At the property Mr Brownlow is at the front door creating a barricade which he believed will stop the bailiff from executing the eviction warrant. Mr Brownlow's next door neighbour, Mr Hayward-Smith who is a member of the housing associations tenant committee, sees the bailiff and the housing officer arrive. He comes out to offer assistance. Mr Hayward-Smith says to the bailiff that if he allows him to speak with Mr Brownlow he will manage to persuade him to come out quietly. The housing officer and the bailiff believe that it is reasonable to allow Mr Hayward-Smith a few moments to speak with Mr Brownlow. While Mr Hayward-Smith is talking with Mr Brownlow the Bailiff decides to call the local police and suggest he may need assistance in executing the warrant. After a few minutes of conversation between Mr Brownlow and Mr Hayward-Smith, Mr Brownlow becomes agitated and starts waving his hands around and using abusive language. He then retreats into the property, closing the door behind him and through the window it can be seen that he has wedged a number of large objects against the door. The bailiff now proceeds to attempt to gain entry upon which Mr Hayward-Smith suggests that it might be easier for the bailiff to attempt entry around the rear of the property. At this point the police arrive and the bailiff, having lost patience with Mr Hayward-Smith discusses the situation with the police who then arrest Hayward-Smith for obstructing a person lawfully acting as an enforcement agent.

In this case of Downton and Mr Brownlow, did Mr Hayward-Smith commit the offence of intentionally obstructing a person lawfully acting as an enforcement agent? The key question here would be whether the actions of Mr Hayward-Smith contained a deliberate intention to make life difficult for the bailiff. He did not intend to make life difficult for the bailiff, as he intended to assist the Bailiff although the actual outcome of his actions was to prejudice the bailiffs success. Therefore, it is likely that Mr Hayward-Smith has not committed the offence of obstructing a bailiff.

However, it is probably not advisable for citizens, even if they are well intentioned, to interfere with a bailiff carrying out his lawful duty.

Interfering with Controlled Goods

Paragraph 68 (2) A in Schedule 12 of the Tribunals, Courts and Enforcement Act 2007 creates an offence of intentionally interfering with controlled goods. Cases have come before the courts on this issue since the new bailiff Regulations came into force in April 2014. In a case in October 2015 at Bromley Magistrates, the debtor removed the clamp placed on the vehicle by the bailiff. He was charged with criminal damage and interfering with controlled goods. He received a fine from the Magistrates Court

****

Part 8

Commercial rent arrears recovery ("CRAR")

Prior to April 2014, landlords of commercial premises who were owed rent by tenants could use a process known as "distress". The advantage of this old common law right was that it was a swift process by which a landlord could take action without having to give, in most cases, notice of the visit by a bailiff.

"Distress" was regarded as unfair to the tenant as the landlord could simply turn up and remove goods. The very fact that bailiffs turned up and removed items was often a sufficient encouragement to the tenant to pay the outstanding rent without the need to actually sell the goods. The new regime of CRAR introduced several measures that provides greater control over the process. There is evidence emerging that CRAR , as was predicted before its introduction, would mean that more commercial tenants will be able to escape this method of recovering rent. Before examining the impact on the recovery of commercial rent, first let's look at the rules of this new procedure.

CRAR

1. It only applies to leases of commercial premises. If any part of the property is occupied as a residential dwelling then it cannot be used.

2. The process can only be used where there is a lease in writing.

3. Only principle rent can be recovered even if the lease reserves sums such as service charges as rent.

4. The process can only be carried out by certified bailiffs.

5. The tenant must be in arrears of at least seven days rent on the date that a bailiff serves notice of intention to exercise CRAR. The notice must give the tenant at least seven clear days notice.

An example of the Notice is given at the end of this Chapter

6. There are restrictions on what can be seized, for example the Bailiff cannot take items necessary for the tenant's personal use in his employment, business or trade such as computer equipment. The restriction applies only to the aggregate value of such items up to £1350. Items over this threshold can be seized.

7. Once the goods have been seized, an inventory must be prepared and given to the tenant by the enforcement agent as soon as is reasonably possible.

8. The goods must be valued in the seven days after they are seized. Once valued, the goods must be disposed of for the best price. A period of seven clear days must expire before a sale can take place.

9. If rights to forfeiture have arisen, then by exercising CRAR these rights are waived.

Example 1

John Anderson design studios rents commercial premises from Frank Brown developments. John Anderson pays rent of £1500 per month for his design studio and there is a flat above the studio which is occupied by an employee of John Anderson as a dwelling. Can Frank Brown use the CRAR process?

No, because some part of the property is occupied as a dwelling.

Example 2

Assume that there is no flat above the studio that is occupied as a dwelling, and John Anderson gets into arrears with his rent. Rent account statement is as follows:

Date	Rent Due	Rent Paid	Balance
1-1-15	£3,000	£3,000	£0
1-2-15	£3,000	£3,000	£0
1-3-15	£3,000	£2,412	£588
1-4-15	£3,000	£3588	£0
1-5-15	£3,000	£2,412	£588
1-6-15	£3,000	£3,588	£0
1-7-15	£3,000	£2,412	£588

On 5 July 2015, Frank Brown Developments serves Notice of intention to recover the rent by using the CRAR process. Is Frank Brown entitled to send in a certified bailiff to seize goods?

The answer is that Frank Brown Development cannot in this example use CRAR. On the surface it may seem perfectly reasonable as a pattern has emerged that John Anderson pays the rent in full one month but then the next month he is short on the payment. The shortfall is paid the following month. When you examine the figures, the actual number of days of rent outstanding when he serves the notice is only 6, and not the required 7.

Example 3

John Anderson is 3 months in arrears when Frank Brown serves a notice of intention to enter the premises. Anxious to recover the rent arrears, Frank Brown instructs the certified bailiff to enter on Friday 17th after having served the Notice on Friday 10th. Will the bailiff be legally entitled to enter on 17th to seize goods?

Frank Brown has not given the correct period of Notice. The period of Notice must be 7 clear days. Where a period includes a Sunday, Bank Holiday or Christmas Day, they are not included in the calculation. In this case, having given notice on Friday 10th, the bailiff could not visit before 19th.

It may seem perfectly reasonable to have a minimum figure of rent outstanding to stop aggressive commercial landlords sending in bailiffs for a very minimal amount.

However as can be seen by example 2 above, there is a pattern of late payment which the tenant is possibly exploiting. Where the monthly rent is higher, six days of unpaid rent would obviously be more significant than in example 2 and so may not seem so small and to the landlord this six days rent could affect his margins quite significantly.

In addition to requiring a minimum of seven days rent outstanding, there is the controversial requirement of having to give at least seven days clear notice before attending. The landlord also faces the hurdle that the bailiff can only enter between the hours of 6am and 9pm, whereas before, entry could be made at any time. The requirement to give notice is controversial for obvious reasons.

The evidence submitted to the Ministry of Justice by the British Property Federation stated that many tenants are using this seven-day notice period as a sort of "cheap overdraft facility". More obviously the concern is that the notice period gives the tenant the opportunity to remove goods, especially where the tenant is in an operation where goods can be easily moved to alternative locations. Although the goods are bound when the notice is received from the certified Bailiff, the reality is that bailiffs have no way of knowing what goods are there when notice was received. In this situation, the phrase "goods being bound" means that with the exception of exempt goods, the goods of the debtor are liable to be taken control of and cannot be assigned or transferred from the date when the notice of enforcement is given.

Challenging CRAR

Not only will the tenant under the new CRAR process be given 7 days notice before attendance, but the tenant also has the right to apply to court under section 78 of the Tribunal Courts and Enforcement Act 2007 to have the Notice set aside or an Order to prevent any further step being taken under CRAR.

The provision in section 78 of the Tribunals, Courts and Enforcement Act 2007 is a useful safeguard to tenants who feel that the landlord is unlawfully or wrongfully seeking to enter to recover rent. An example of when a tenant might be able to take advantage of this provision is set out below.

Example

Fine Teas is a cafe business that occupies premises in the High Street of Upmarket. The landlord is a company called Ratman Properties. Fine Teas have a lease under which they pay £5000 per quarter. The lease contains covenants that obliges the landlord to maintain and repair the external structure of the building. The property is affected by water leaks and this impacts on the business of buying teas. They miss a payment of rent and the landlord then decides to instruct a bailiff to serve a notice of enforcement in respect of commercial rent arrears recovery.

In this example, Fine Teas might be able to take advantage of section 78 of the Act so as to prevent any further steps being taken under CRAR. It would need to make an application to the court to either have the notice set aside or to stop further steps. Fine Teas would have to argue that they are entitled to set-off rent against compensation which might be payable by Ratman Properties by reason of damage caused by the water leaks. The amount of compensation would depend on the circumstances and so it is not certain a court would grant an Order preventing further steps.

****

COMMERCIAL RENT ARREARS RECOVERY: NOTICE OF ENFORCEMENT

NOTICE TO TENANT UNDER PARAGRAPH 7(1) OF SCHEDULE 12 TO THE TRIBUNALS, COURTS AND ENFORCEMENT ACT 2007

To: <<Tenant's name(s)>>
       <<Address>>
       <<Address>>
       <<Postcode>>

From: <<Enforcement Agent's name>> ("Enforcement Agent")
       <<Address>>
       <<Address>>
       <<Postcode>>

1. This Notice relates to the property known as <<Full address of property>> ("Property").

2. You are the tenant of the Property under a lease dated <<date>> between (1) <<Origina Landlord>> and (2) <<Original Tenant>> ("Lease").

3. Your landlord is <<Landlord's name>> ("Landlord").

4. The Landlord has the right to recover rent arrears from you by commercial rent arrears recovery under section 72(1) of the Tribunals, Courts and Enforcement Act 2007.

5. You owe the Landlord rent of £<<amount>> ("Rent").

6. The rent is owed in respect of the period from <<date>> to <<date>>.

7. As at the date of this Notice you also owe the Landlord interest on the unpaid rent amounting to £<<amount>> ("Interest").

8. The enforcement costs incurred by the Landlord up to the date of this Notice are £<<amount>> ("Enforcement Costs").

9. The possible additional costs of enforcement if the Rent, Interest and Enforcement Costs should remain unpaid as at the time and date specified in paragraph 12 below are £<<amount>>.

10. Payment of the Rent, Interest and Enforcement Costs may be made by <<e.g. cash, cheque made payable to xxx, bank transfer to sort code xx-xx-xx account number xxxxxxxx>>. Payment may be made in person at <<address>> between the hours of <<e.g. 9am and 5pm>> on <<e.g. Monday to Friday (inclusive)>>.

11. The Enforcement Agent or the Enforcement Agent's office may be contacted on <<telephone number>> or at <<email address>> between the hours of <<e.g. 9am and 5pm>> on <<e.g. Monday to Friday (inclusive)>>. Written correspondence may be sent to <<address>>.

12. The Rent, Interest and Enforcement Costs must be paid by <<time>> on <<date>> to prevent goods belonging to you being taken control of and sold and your incurring additional costs.

116

Part 9

Removal and sale by a bailiff

The majority of cases where the bailiff has taken control of goods will lead to an instalment arrangement. The new Regulations will provide two opportunities for an arrangement to be made, upon receipt of the Notice of Enforcement and later under a Controlled Goods Agreement.

It may well be that the creditor and debtor cannot agree an arrangement. The Taking Control of Goods: National Standards, provides guidance in respect of instalments:

24. Debtors must not be pressed to make unrealistic offers and should be asked to consider carefully any offer they voluntarily make and where possible refer to free debt advice.

25. Where a creditor has indicated they will accept a reasonable repayment offer, enforcement agents must refer such offers onto the creditor.

Removal and sale should be considered the last resort. It may be necessary for the bailiff to force entry to premises in order to check on the goods that have been taken into control or to remove them for sale. The bailiff has the power to use reasonable force where the goods have been taken into control. This right of re-entry is covered by paragraph 16 of Schedule 12, which is set out below. The NSEA warns about using the power of forced entry and it should be used only where reasonably required and after the debtor has been told that it will be used.

Re-entry

16   (1)   This paragraph applies where goods on any premises have been taken control of and have not been removed by the enforcement agent.

(2)   The enforcement agent may enter the premises to inspect the goods or to remove them for storage or sale.

(3)   This paragraph authorises repeated entry to the same premises.

When a bailiff returns to re-enter, the regulations about the day and time also apply to re-entering. So the bailiff may re-enter on any day of the week and between the hours of 6am and 9pm unless the goods are located on premises that are either wholly or partly used for business and those premises are open for business outside those hours. In addition to the rules about the days and time, the re-entry should only be made through a normal access route and the bailiff should not re-enter if a child or vulnerable person is the only one present on the premises.

Before a bailiff re-enters to remove goods after a breach of a controlled goods order, a Notice of intention to re-enter must be given to the debtor with not less than 2 clear days warning of the intended visit (not counting Sundays, bank holidays, Good Friday or Christmas day). The period of notice can be shortened, but the bailiff would have to apply to the court (without notice of the application to the debtor) and satisfy the judge that if the shorter time period was permitted, the debtor might move the goods.

When goods are removed from premises by the bailiff for the purposes of sale, a signed Notice must be provided to the debtor and the Notice must contain the following:

- The fact that goods have been removed for storage or sale
- A list of items removed if this is different from those listed after taking control
- The date of the removal for sale
- The procedure for making payment so as to prevent the sale of goods

The prescribed form for giving the above information is shown at the end of this Chapter.

The care of controlled goods

If a bailiff removes goods, they should be kept in the same condition as they were when they were found. The bailiff must take care of the controlled goods and the standard of care is regarded as being the same degree of care that would be expected to be exercised by a person of reasonable judgment over his/her own property. If the goods are stored at an auction house, the auctioneer must exercise reasonable care and skill in keeping them and is liable for any damage or loss arising from his default or negligence. The auctioneer being in possession of the goods has an interest in the goods which entitles him to sue for trespass if anybody tries to interfere or the debtor attempts to recover the goods. Consider the case example below of "Distinguished Auctioneers".

Distinguished Auctioneers and Fred Smith

Fred Smith has had his goods removed by the High Court Enforcement Officer for the failure to pay a judgment debt in the sum of £15,000 owed to Gary Pratt. High

Court Enforcement company, "Take Away Ltd", removed goods from Fred Smith after he breached the terms of a controlled goods agreement and took them to Distinguished Auctioneers. The goods that Take Away removed included antique furniture believed to be worth about £20,000. The Notice that goods had been removed for sale explained that if Mr Smith made full payment to the bailiff the goods could be collected. Seven days after the goods were removed to Distinguished, Mr Smith attends the offices of Take Away Ltd and produces a banker's draft for the full Judgment Debt and costs. Take Away then contact Distinguished to make the arrangements for Fred Smith to collect his property. However, Distinguished say that the previous day the items were stolen from their premises! It transpires that Distinguished Antiques had stored the antique furniture in a shed in the yard at the back of their shop with no lock on it and the gate to the yard also had no lock on it. When Mr Smith is told, he is very angry and seeks legal advice.

Fred Smith, the debtor in the above case, would have the basis to bring a claim against the bailiff under paragraph 66 of Schedule 12 to TCE 2007. A bailiff is able to take controlled goods direct to an auctioneer provided it is secure and suitable, ensuring that there will not be damage or deterioration to the goods. The facts of Distinguished and Fred Smith do make you question whether Take Away made proper checks to ensure that the goods would be secure at the premises of Distinguished Auctioneers. It should have been apparent that the unlocked "shed" was not a secure place to store the antique furniture. Therefore, it would seem that the bailiff was negligent and Fred Smith would be able to seek damages from Take Away.

Sale

There is a general obligation on the bailiff to sell or dispose of controlled goods for the best price that can reasonably be obtained. To help achieve the best price, immediately after the removal of goods the bailiff must obtain a valuation of the controlled goods and give the debtor and any co-owner the opportunity to obtain an independent valuation. There is no prescribed form for the bailiff to use to inform the debtor about valuation but it must state that a valuation will be undertaken and that the debtor and co-owner is permitted to arrange their own.

The valuation must be in writing and should be signed by the enforcement agent. The valuation should be dated with the bailiff's reference number. A copy should be provided to the debtor and any co-owner.

The reason for the valuation is related to the duty of the bailiff to avoid excessive levies and re-iterates the requirement for the bailiff to ensure that there is proportionality between the value of the goods taken into control and debt and costs due.

Although the debtor has the right to obtain a valuation, there is no specified procedure for resolving disputes about the valuation. Having said that, paragraph 66 of Schedule 12 of the TCE Act 2007 does provide remedies for the debtor. Paragraph 66 applies where the enforcement agent has breached any of the provisions in Schedule 12 and paragraph 66 (5) provides a remedy of damages for a loss suffered as a result of the breach of the provisions. In a case of not obtaining the best price, an application could be made under paragraph 66 arguing that there has been a breach of paragraph 37 which states:

"Best price

37(1)An enforcement agent must sell or dispose of controlled goods for the best price that can reasonably be obtained in accordance with this Schedule.

(2)That does not apply to money that can be used for paying any of the outstanding amount, unless the best price is more than its value if used in that way."

Notice of Sale

This also something that is new. The bailiff is required to give the debtor and any co-owner a notice of the date, time and place of the sale. The notice period is a minimum of 7 clear days. If the goods are perishable, notice can be given the day before. The notice must contain:

- The name and address of the debtor and any co-owner
- The bailiff's name and reference
- That the sale is conditional upon a satisfactory purchaser. An offer must at least cover the reserve price which is assumed to be the valuation

- The amount of the debt due including costs at the date of the notice
- How and when payment may be made to prevent sale
- Where payment is made, how the goods can be collected by the debtor/co-owner

A copy of the prescribed form for giving Notice of Sale is shown at the end of this Chapter.

The method of sale must be by public auction unless the court orders otherwise. The court can only order a different method of sale upon receipt of an application from the enforcement agent. There are four alternative methods of sale which may be permitted by the court;

- Private contract
- Sealed bids
- Advertisement, or
- Such other method as the court thinks fit

The application by the enforcement agent for an alternative sale method must state whether he/she believes another enforcement power has become exercisable by another creditor. If the application states it is believed another bailiff is instructed then notice of the application must be given to that other creditor.

Place and conduct of the sale

Generally, the sale should take place at a public auction. A sale may though take place on the premises of the debtor where the goods were found if the premises are used solely for trade purposes and the debtor gives consent. If necessary, the enforcement agent may use reasonable force to enable the sale to take place and any person to enter. On leaving after the sale, the bailiff must leave the premises as secure as he found them.

The Taking Control of Goods Regulations 2013 provide little guidance on the conduct of the sale. All that Regulation 43 says is as follows:

Conduct of sale

43. Where controlled goods are sold by public auction, the auction must be conducted by—
(a)a qualified auctioneer; or
(b)where the auction takes place online or on an internet auction site, an auction provider independent of the enforcement agent.

So it would seem that the Regulations will rely on the professionalism of the auction providers. However, to understand what is not likely to be allowed, the case law before the current Regulations may give some guidance. Under the old law, a sale of some description had to take place and the goods could not be handed over to the creditor; the creditor and debtor could buy them at the sale. If the goods are of a specialist nature, the bailiff might obtain advice on the mode of sale. Having the provision that a valuation must be obtained provides guidance and a safeguard that the goods will be sold at the best price. The cases prior to the new Regulations indicate a number of types of claim for mishandling a sale could be brought, these include:

- Mishandling the goods

124

- Mishandling the sale
- Failing properly to advertise the sale
- Delaying the sale
- Selling too much

If the bailiff is unable to find buyers for the goods, he would not be negligent provided he can show that he made sufficient efforts to sell the goods before voluntarily abandoning goods of sufficient value. The term "abandoning goods" is defined in paragraph 52 of Schedule 12. It relates to where a notice of sale is not given in respect of control goods within 12 months of taking control or where goods remain unsold after giving a notice of sale. The consequences of goods being abandoned is that enforcement powers cease to be exercisable and also the bailiff must make the goods available for collection if they were removed from where they were found.

What if the goods are sold for greatly under their value?

As we have seen above, paragraph 37 requires the bailiff to obtain the best possible price. If the debtor believes that the bailiff has not complied with the rules as to sale then a claim can be brought under Schedule 12, paragraph 66. The example below concerns a debtor alleging the best price was not obtained.

Mr Spotter v. Carefree Bailiffs

Carefree bailiffs removed controlled goods from Mr Spotter. They took the vintage and rather rare steam engine to Upmarket Auctions. The auction was advertised in the usual way which was in the local press. The auction attracted relatively few bidders and the engine was eventually sold at the auction for £20,000. Mr Spotter argued that the bailiff had not obtained the best price for the steam engine. In response, the bailiff argued that this was the price realised at the public auction and that this was evidence of the value of the steam engine.

The circumstances in the example of **Mr Spotter** does lend itself to the fact that the best price may not have been obtained. The price obtained at an auction is not always the best evidence of the value of goods at a particular date but the Judge may accept this evidence of its value in the absence of other evidence. The onus would be on the person alleging it was not sold at the best price to produce evidence to show a substantial difference between the price realised and the value on that date. In the case of **Mr Spotter**, it would appear that the vintage steam engine is an item of a specialist nature and we would need to know what steps were taken to obtain specialist advice about the mode of sale. If proper advice about the sale had not been taken, such as not advertising in specialist magazines to encourage bids, then it might show that not all reasonable steps had been taken to obtain the best price.

The point about taking specialist advice in the sale of items was made in the case of **American Express International Banking Corporation -v- Hurley (1985).** The case concerned mortgaged property and a company that specialised in sound and lighting equipment used at pop concerts. The mortgagee's guarantor was dissatisfied with the way in which the receiver sold the equipment. The court decided that there was a failure to take reasonable care in selling the equipment because there was:

(i) a failure to take specialist advice from a person in the popular music industry;

(ii) a failure to advertise in publications concerning the popular music industry. The receiver is liable in negligence to the guarantor.

Proceeds of Sale

The proceeds of sale must be used to pay the amount outstanding. If the proceeds are less than the amount outstanding, the distribution is set out in Regulation 13 of the 2014 Fee Regulations as follows:

- co-owners,
- the auctioneers,
- the bailiff's compliance fee (currently £75),
- bailiff & creditor then take a pro-rata share of balance

Regulation 13 is a change from the previous position where the bailiff had a priority claim to the recovery of his fees.

If proceeds of sale are greater than the amount outstanding, the surplus must be paid to the debtor. If there is a co-owner, the bailiff must first pay the co-owner their share according to their interest and then distribute as set out above. If there is a dispute about the share to be paid to the co-owner, an application to the court can be made to determine the matter.

****

Notice of intention to re-enter premises

This notice must be given by the enforcement agent or the enforcement agent's office.

Warning If necessary the enforcement agent may use reasonable force to re-enter your premises to inspect your goods or remove them for storage or sale.

Please read this notice - it is important

Name of Debtor

Address

Date notice issued [ ] [ ] / [ ] [ ] / [ ] [ ] [ ] [ ] .

Enforcement agent reference number

About this notice You have been given this notice of intention to re-enter because you have not kept to the repayment terms of the controlled goods agreement and the enforcement agent now intends to re-enter your premises to inspect your goods or remove them for storage or sale.

Who you owe money to

The amount you owe them

Their ref./account no.
(if applicable)

Enforcement details Details of the court judgment or order or enforcement power by virtue of which the debt is enforceable.

Controlled goods agreement Details of the controlled goods agreement which you have failed to keep to:

Repayment details

Details of how you have failed to keep to the repayment terms of this controlled goods agreement:

Sum outstanding

Debt [ ]

Interest [ ]

Compliance stage fee [ ]

Enforcement stage fee

TOTAL sum outstanding [ ]

(as at the date of this notice)

When to make payment

You must pay this amount by:

Date [ ][ ]/[ ][ ]/[ ][ ][ ][ ]

Time [ ]

If you do not pay

If you do not pay by the date above, an enforcement agent will re-enter your premises to inspect your belongs or to remove them for storage or sale. These actions will increase the costs of enforcement and these costs will be added to the amount already owed.

Possible additional fees and expenses of enforcement

If the sum outstanding remains unpaid by the date and time above you may be charged the following (enforcement agent to detail further possible fees and expenses).

How to pay what you owe

How to pay including opening hours and days

How you can contact the enforcement agent or the enforcement agent's office

Telephone

Address

Opening hours and days

Signature

Enforcement Agent

PRINT NAME

You can seek free advice and information from

AdviceUK at www.adviceuk.org.uk/find-a-member

National Debtline at www.nationaldebtline.org or on 0808 808 4000

Money Advice Service at www.moneyadviceservice.org.uk or on 0300 500 5000

Gov.uk at www.gov.uk

Other free advice is available.

131

Notice that goods have been removed for storage or sale

About this notice   This is to tell you that I have removed the goods listed at the back of this notice to secure storage or for sale.

Enforcement details   Details of the court judgment or order or enforcement power by virtue of which the debt is enforceable.

Date and time of removal

Date ☐☐ / ☐☐ / ☐☐☐☐

Time ☐

I have done this because you have not paid the sum outstanding.

Daily or weekly storage charge payable where goods removed to storage

Sum outstanding

Debt

Interest

Compliance stage fee

Enforcement stage fee

Sale stage fee

Expenses (if any)   Please detail the expenses

TOTAL sum outstanding

(as at the date of this notice)

**How to pay
what you owe**

How to pay including opening hours and days

**How to collect
your goods**

If you pay the amount you owe, you will be able to collect your goods by (describe procedure in
bullet point form)

Signature

Enforcement Agent

PRINT NAME

**You can seek
free advice and
information
from**

AdviceUK at www.adviceuk.org.uk/find-a-member

National Debtline at www.nationaldebtline.org or on 0808 808 4000

Money Advice Service at www.moneyadviceservice.org.uk or on 0300 500 5000

Gov.uk at www.gov.uk

Other free advice is available.

133

Notice of sale

Please read this notice - it is important

Name of Debtor

Address

Date notice issued

Enforcement agent reference number

Name of enforcement agent

Name of co-owner (if applicable)

Address of co-owner (if applicable)

Enforcement details

Details of the court judgment or order or enforcement power by virtue of which the debt is enforceable

Because you have not paid the sum outstanding *(detailed over the page)*, **the goods listed at the back of this notice may be sold.**

Sum outstanding

Debt [   ]

Interest [   ]

Compliance stage fee [   ]

Enforcement stage fee
or fees, if High Court
enforcement [   ]

Sale stage fee [   ]

Expenses (if any) [   ]

Please detail the expenses

[   ]

**TOTAL sum
outstanding** [   ]

(as at the date of this notice)

**Date, time and
place of sale**

The sale will take place on

Date [ ]/[ ]/[   ]   Time [   ]

Address [   ]

**When to make
payment**

To avoid goods taken into control being sold the sum outstanding must be paid by

Date [ ]/[ ]/[   ]

Time [   ]

**How to pay
what you owe**

How to pay including opening hours and days

[   ]

How to collect your goods

If you pay the amount you owe, you will be able to collect your goods by
(describe procedure in bullet point form)

Signature

....

Enforcement Agent

....

PRINT NAME

You can seek free advice and information from

AdviceUK at www.adviceuk.org.uk/find-a-member

National Debtline at www.nationaldebtline.org or 0808 808 4000

Money Advice Service at www.moneyadviceservice.org.uk or on 0300 500 5000

Gov.uk at www.gov.uk

Other free advice is available.

136

Part 10

Bailiff Fees

The changes introduced by the TCE 2007 will undoubtedly have a major impact on enforcement agents. From speaking to those in the industry, some of the major players in the sector are diversifying into other sectors as the changes to bailiff fees will have a major impact on the profitability of providing enforcement services. Some High Court Enforcement organisations have moved into linked areas such as security services and have bought/set up law firms that can offer the complete debt recovery package from the initial instruction to chase a debt through to legal action and the enforcement of judgments.

Paragraph 62 of schedule 12 in the Tribunals, Courts and Enforcement Act 2007 sets out the broad principles for the charging of fees by bailiffs. The Taking Control of Goods (Fees) Regulations 2014 provides detail. The new fee Regulations take a totally different but simple approach to the calculation of daily fees. The fees are either fixed or calculated as a percentage of the sum to be recovered which is described as debt which remains unpaid or the amount that the creditor agrees to accept in satisfaction of the debt.

The new fee structure for enforcement agents is summarised below:

Non High Court Enforcement

Stage	Fixed fee	% Fee (of sum to be recovered)
Compliance	£75.00	0%
Enforcement	£235.00	7.5%
Sale or Disposal	£110.00	7.5%

High Court Enforcement

Stage	Fixed fee	% Fee (of sum to be recovered)
Compliance	£75.00	0%
1st Enforcement	£190.00	7.5%
2nd Enforcement	£495.00	0%
Sale Stage	£525.00	7.5%

High Court Enforcement:

Compliance Stage

The process starts with the Compliance stage. All High Court Enforcement companies will have to send a 'Notice of Enforcement' to the judgment debtor.

This notice gives them 7 clear days, excluding Sundays and bank holidays, to make payment in full to prevent the attendance of an Enforcement Agent (EA) to seize goods.

The new term replacing seizure is 'take control of goods', and the Writ of fieri facias is to be renamed the

Writ of control. Sending the Notice of Enforcement triggers the fee for this stage which is £75.

Enforcement Stage 1

If the debtor fails to make contact with the HCEO or requests to pay by instalments during the Compliance Stage, an Enforcement Agent ("EA") will attend their premises to take control of goods.

This stage is known as Enforcement Stage 1 and the fixed charge at this point is £190 plus 7.5% of the sums to be recovered over £1,000. For example, if the outstanding debt was £3,000, the 7.5% would only be charged on £2,000. The sums to be recovered are the judgment debt, court costs and execution costs.

If, when the EA attends, the debtor pays in full immediately or agrees to an acceptable instalment arrangement, then the matter ends there.

Enforcement Stage 2

If the debtor refuses either to make any payment or to enter into an acceptable instalment arrangement covered by a controlled goods agreement (the term replacing walking possession agreement), then the matter moves to Enforcement Stage 2. If a payment arrangement, with a signed controlled goods agreement, is subsequently broken, the Enforcement Agent will re-attend the property either under Enforcement Stage 2 or the Sales or Disposal Stage, depending upon the circumstances so far. The fee for Enforcement Stage 2 is a flat £495.

Sale or Disposal Stage

Should enforcement get to the point where goods actually need to be removed, the enforcement progresses to the Sale or Disposal Stage.

The fee for this stage is £525 plus 7.5% of the outstanding debt over £1,000. The costs of removal are normally included in this Sale Stage fee.

However, if the HCEO anticipates exceptionally high removal costs far greater than the Sale Stage fee, for example specialist equipment and personnel to remove an aircraft, he can apply to the court to have these added to the amount payable by the debtor.

Disbursements

Bailiffs are also permitted to claim limited out-of-pocket expenses from the debtor. Regulation 8 states that expenses may be recovered provided they are reasonable and actually incurred. These include:

- The cost of storing goods taken into control
- Cost of hiring a locksmith
- Court fees payable for any applications made by the bailiff in relation to the enforcement powers which the application is granted. The cost of an application to court can be passed onto the debtor provided the application is successful.

Disbursement costs for the expense of conducting a sale or disposal of assets that are seized by a bailiff can be recovered in addition to the prescribed scale fee where a sale is held on premises provided by the auctioneer conducting the sale. The bailiff may recover:

- The auctioneers commission not exceeding 15% of the sum realised by the sale

- The auctioneers out-of-pocket expenses

- Reasonable expenses incurred in advertising sale

If the sale is held on other premises the bailiff may recover from the debtor the same expenses which are set out above except the auctioneer's commission is limited to 7.5% of the sum realised by sale.

Vulnerable debtors

If the debtor is a vulnerable person the fee or fees due for the enforcement stages and any related expenses are not recoverable from the debtor unless the enforcement agent has given the person adequate opportunity to obtain assistance and advice before the goods are removed

The new abortive fee

The current abortive fee, payable if enforcement proves to be unsuccessful, will rise from £60 to £75. This fee is triggered by the sending of the Notice of

Enforcement and is payable by the creditor in the case of unsuccessful enforcement.

Liability for charges

The new regulations state what the bailiff is permitted to recover. Where the sum recovered by the bailiff is less than the total debt outstanding the sequence for applying the money is specified in Regulation 13 of the Taking Control of Goods (Fees) Regulations 2014. Any fees and expenses owed to an auctioneer and the compliance stage fee for the enforcement agent are prioritised, with the remaining proceeds being divided pro rata between payment of the debt and payment of the remaining fees and disbursements due to the enforcement agent.

The above rules are not the same if the full debt is recovered, although co-owners rights will always be given preferential treatment. The regulations make clear that these expenses cannot be recovered where the enforcement process has ceased.

Challenging fees

In order to be able to contest the fee the debtor will obviously need to have evidence upon which to base the challenge. Under the new regulations, there will be various notices provided to the debtor with information about the sums due and the accruing fees. Also there is a duty on the bailiff to provide a final account to the debtor after the sale or disposal of goods giving a breakdown of the distribution of proceeds.

If there are disputes about fees, matters can be taken up with the bailiff company and also the creditor. If is not possible to resolve the dispute there are a number of options available. Complaints can be made to the relevant trade body or to an appropriate ombudsman. A large number of complaints about local authority bailiffs have concerned disputes over fees. Overcharging and not complying with the regulations have been considered on a number of occasions by the ombudsman for local government, and where the complaints that have been upheld have required the amounts to be repaid and compensation be awarded.

The new regulations provide that in the event of a dispute regarding the amount recoverable under the regulations, the sum claimed may be assessed in accordance with the rules of court. This refers to an assessment being made by the court. A debtor disputing the enforcement agents bill can apply to the court if there is dispute about the amount of fees or disbursements or exceptional disbursements and party wishes the court to determine the amount lawfully recoverable. The application is made to the court on form N244 and must be accompanied by evidence.

A debtor who is disputing a charge could make a claim to the County Court. The debtor's course of action would be to pay the disputed bailiff and then issue a claim to recover this and any sums that are alleged to have been wrongfully paid on the grounds that they were paid under coercion. It is argued that duress in this respect relates to a person paying money to the bailiff through fear of their property being wrongfully seized or detained. The debtor must make clear that they are paying under protest. Establishing that payment was made under protest is important because seizure under a warrant is not illegal pressure and any payment made by the debtor to release goods is simply submission to that legal process. So money paid to release goods in the custody of the bailiff is not paid under duress and cannot be recovered. Therefore there must be some wrongful element in the levy and the debtor in paying was retaining use of the goods rather than being deprived of them during lengthy court proceedings.

In the case of Maskell v Horner **[1915] 3 KB 106,** the defendant demanded money from the claimant by way of a 'toll fee' for his market stall. The defendant had no legal basis for demanding this money. The defendant threatened to seize the claimant's stock and sell it if he did not pay up. The claimant paid the toll fee for a considerable period of time and then brought an action to recover the money paid under duress. The court held that the claimant was entitled to recover the sums paid in the law of restitution.

****

Part 11

Overall Summary of New Bailiff Laws

The new bailiff laws represent a significant change from the previous rules. The new statutory regime is a very prescriptive process and it puts a high degree of responsibility on the bailiffs to ensure that the taking control of goods is carried out correctly. Bailiffs will need higher levels of training and accuracy and it is imperative that they serve the correct notices and follow the correct procedures at each stage.

It is obvious from all the new requirements to serve notices on debtors that the process will take much longer than it did in the past. The key requirement is that the debtor must be informed of what is going on at each stage with the correct notice. Obviously, giving notice to debtors of the enforcement process before the bailiff attends will give away the advantage that High Court Enforcement Agents had in the past because they were able to turn up unannounced. Cynics will say that this giving of notice before the bailiff attends is too heavily in favour of the debtor who will have time to remove goods.

Although in legal terms the goods of the debtor become "bound" at the point they are given notice, the prescribed enforcement notice does not make any mention of the binding effect of receiving the notice so debtors are not warned against improper dealings with their goods once they have been given notice of enforcement.

The new bailiff rules require notices to be given at each stage of this enforcement process. The notices that are required to be given include:

- enforcement notice warning the debtor a warrant or writ has been issued
- notice after entry
- notice after taking control of goods
- copies of control goods agreements
- notice after removal of goods from premises
- notice before sale or disposal of goods

If the bailiff fails to provide the correct statutory notice then it may invalidate subsequent stages of the process. This greater administrative burden on the bailiff will add further costs to the enforcement process. With the introduction of a much simplified fixed fee scale it will undoubtedly impact on the business of bailiff companies and it is not surprising that some High Court enforcement companies have diversified into other areas of work such as becoming regulated as an "Alternative Business Structure" ("ABS") to enable them to operate in the provision of legal services. An ABS is a regulated organisation which provides legal services and has some form of non-lawyer involvement.

The key thing that debtors want to know when a bailiff arrives is do they have the power to force entry? The answer will depend on the type of debt that is being enforced. Bailiffs/enforcement agents are allowed to force entry to enforce criminal court fines and if they have obtained peaceful entry before and they are returning to remove goods or to check up on goods taken into control. In addition, reasonable force can be used to gain entry if the judgment debtor is a business and it is believed the debtor carries on a trade or business from the premises. Before the new rules were formulated, there was talk that the right to force entry would be extended but after representations from various interested parties that did not happen. It would have been seen as a step too far by many to allow bailiffs to force entry into residential premises on their first visit.

The new regulations make it clear that entry to premises is only possible through the usual means of entry which means by doors and gates or similar entrances. This does away with the previous rule that permitted bailiffs to enter through an open window.

In addition to the change about the means of entry, there is now a more comprehensive list of what goods are exempt from being taken into control by the bailiff. The exemption list for household goods has increased significantly. So the range of goods which a bailiff may take into control has become more restricted, whilst at the same time they are expected to take more care when deciding which goods they can take control of.

When they do take goods into control, such as through a controlled goods agreement, the inventory that goes with the Notice must be more specific about the description of the goods.

Regulation 33 of the Taking Control of Goods Regulations 2013 states:

(e) a list of the goods of which control has been taken with a description to enable the debtor or the co-owner to identify the goods correctly, including, where applicable—

    (i) the manufacturer, model and serial number of the goods;

    (ii) in the case of a vehicle, the manufacturer, model, colour and registration mark of the vehicle; and

    (iii) the material, colour and usage, and (where appropriate) any other identifying characteristic, of the goods.

Regulation 33 will mean that the description of the goods on the inventory will be less vague. Of course this will add to the time it takes a bailiff to accomplish the process of taking control of goods. All this will increase a bailiff company's costs.

Not only is the serving of additional notices creating a larger administrative burden on bailiffs, but the increased training and regulation will add further cost implications. The Certification of Enforcement Agents Regulations 2014 set out the application process and competency requirements for an individual to demonstrate that they should be certificated to act as an enforcement agent. The competencies include being able to demonstrate to a judge that he possesses sufficient knowledge of the law and procedure relating to the powers under the Tribunals Courts and Enforcement Act 2007. The Committee in Parliament that considers statutory instruments queried the absence of a definition of vulnerability and the way training enforcement agents in these situations can be implemented.

Training packages focusing on vulnerability issues have been developed by the Royal College of psychiatrists and the money advice trust in consultation with the Civil Enforcement Association to support applicants who are applying for certification. The packages include training on how agents should deal with individuals who may be vulnerable. They offer courses where trainees can practice different techniques for dealing with vulnerable individuals when recovering debt. There are also E-learning courses that raise awareness of mental health.

The High Court Enforcement Officers Association has an education program for those who wish to train to become a High Court Enforcement Officer. Students have to be at a certain educational level in law and credit management issues to start the programme. If the educational qualifications are accepted then the Association will accept the applicant as a student member and so begin on the training path to becoming an Associate Member. An Associate member can apply to the Lord Chancellor for full authorisation as a High Court enforcement officer. An authorised High Court enforcement officer can execute judgments and other orders of the High Court and County Court of England and Wales.

The bailiff is expected to take reasonable enquiries to determine whether or not a person has a claim over goods taken into control. If a third party believes that he owns the goods that have been taken by the bailiff, there is a procedure for that third party to claim the restoration of their property. The one major hurdle placed on third parties though is the fact that if the creditor disputes his claim to ownership, when the third party makes the application to the court, he is required to pay a proportion of the value of the goods in addition to the court fee payable to issue the application. With court fees expected to increase, this in itself front loads costs onto the third party claimant and with the requirement to pay a proportion of the value of the goods, this burden is even greater.

The new regulations require that whenever goods are removed from premises for storage or sale, the goods must be valued by the bailiff and a copy of the valuation be provided to the debtor and any co-owners. The likely consequences of this is that it will increase expenses to be met from the new fixed fees for the final stage of the enforcement process and will add delay to the overall process. The new regulations have created a much simplified fee scale. Bailiff fees over the years generated many disputes. It is expected that the new simpler fee structure system will reduce the number of disputes over bailiff fees.

Conclusion

The overall message of the new bailiff law is that every stage of the process requires the appropriate notice to be given to the debtor. This along with simpler and fixed fees has tipped the pendulum back in favour of the debtor. Bailiff companies are faced with higher costs and a reduced prospect of recovering debts because the unscrupulous debtor will be able to put goods out of reach because of the advanced warning of visits. The creditor will be faced with less chance of recovering debts through the use of a bailiff and with the increased costs of regulation imposed on bailiff companies, they will probably be only interested in the larger providers of instructions and also debts that will prove easier to recover.

USEFUL SOURCES OF FURTHER INFOMATION

Useful website on bailiff law:

Bailiff Advice Online: www.bailiffadviceonline.co.uk

Popular website providing up to date and accurate information regarding the enforcement of debts by bailiffs/enforcement agents. It is used daily by members of the public, advice centres, local authorities, magistrates courts and county courts, solicitors, and even police officers.

Legislation.gov.uk:

Official Government Site containing all Acts of Parliament and Statutory Instruments

High Court Enforcement Companies:

High Court Enforcement Group Ltd: www.hcegroup.co.uk

The Marston Group: www.marstongroup.co.uk

Shergroup Enforcement:www.shergroup.net/enforcement

Andrew Wilson & Co: www.andrewwilsonandco.com

Associations:

High Court Enforcement Association: www.hceoa.org.uk
Civil Enforcement Association: www.civea.co.uk

Index